Farting Unicorns

Color Test Page

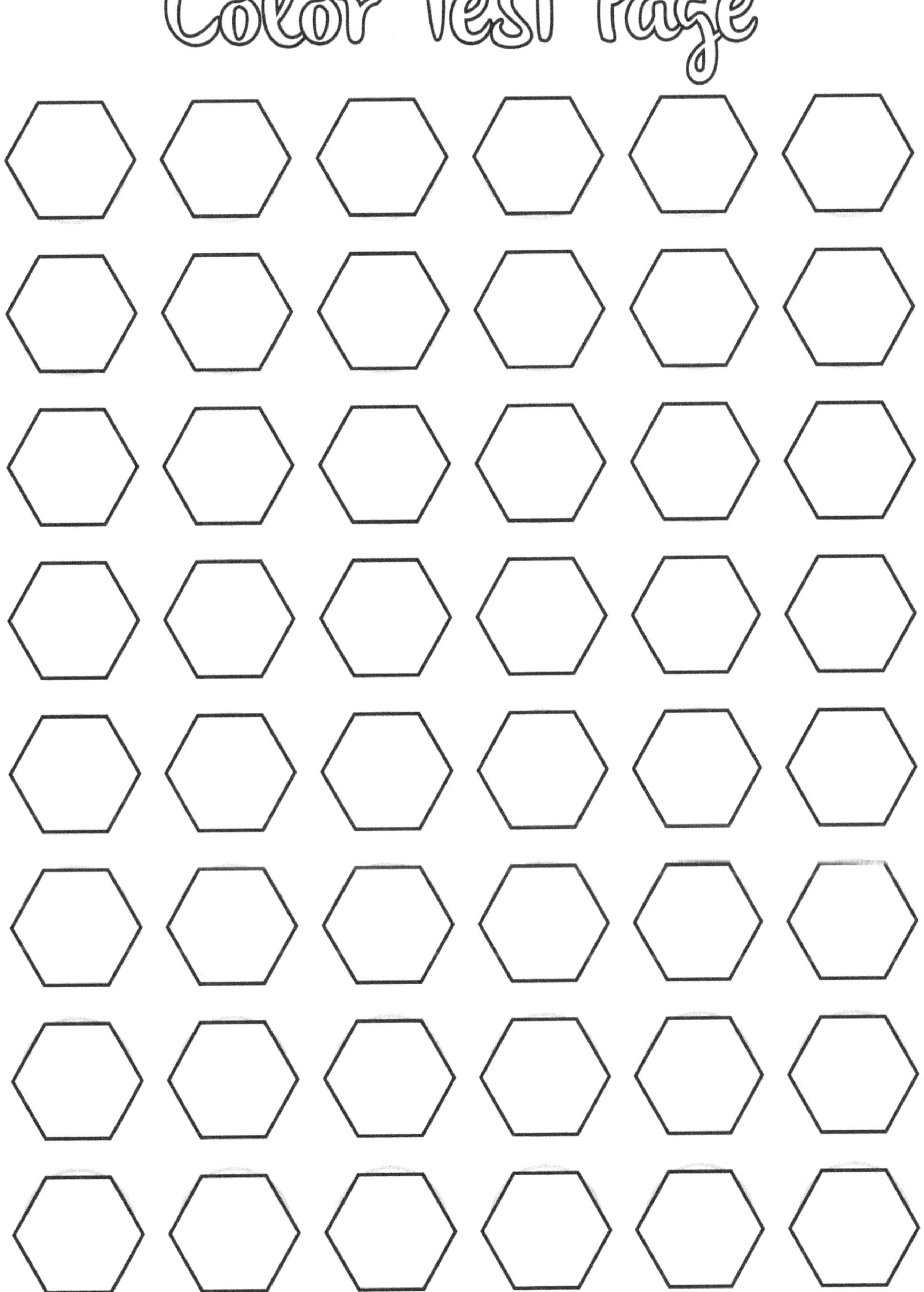

Color Test Page

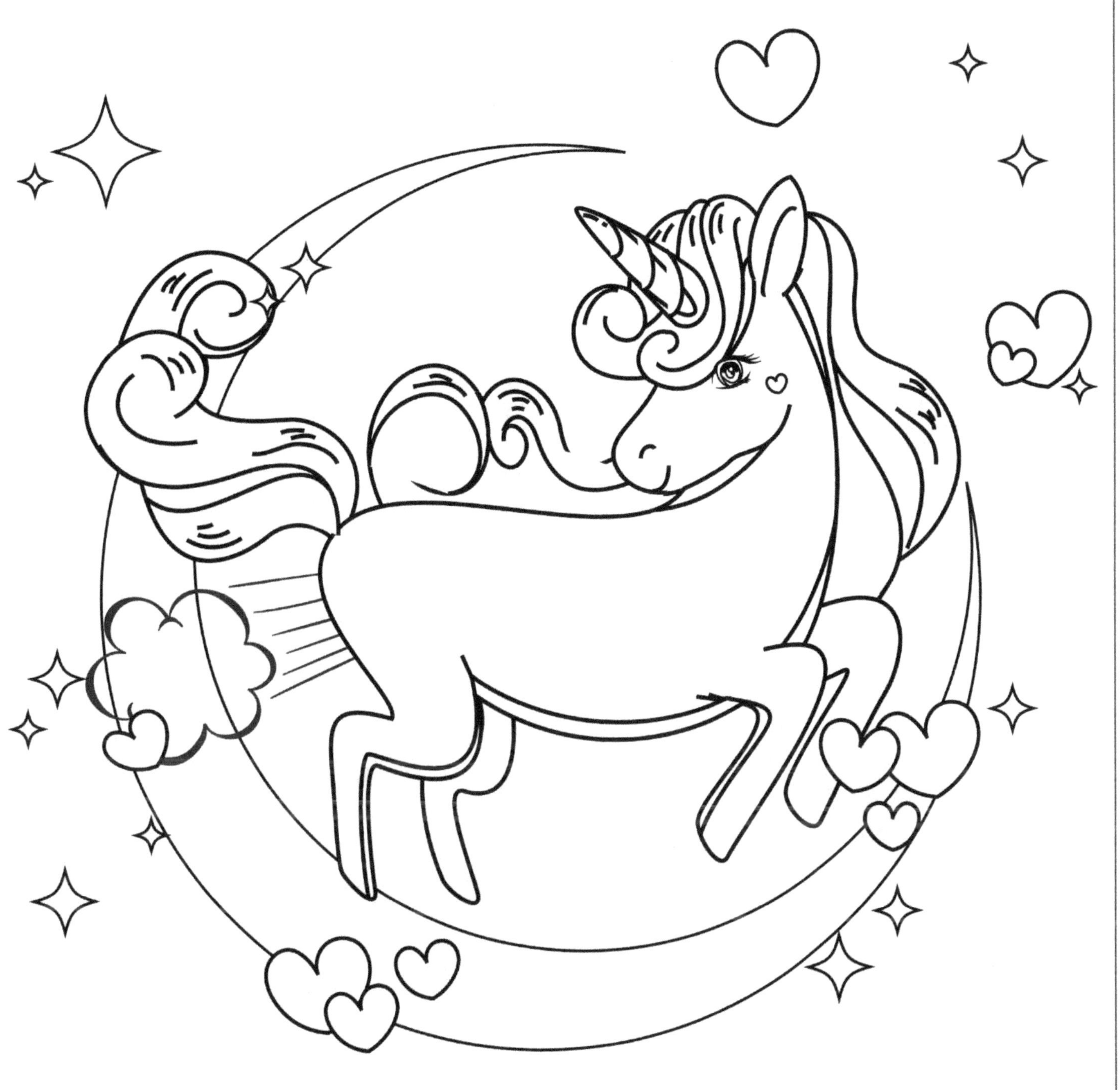

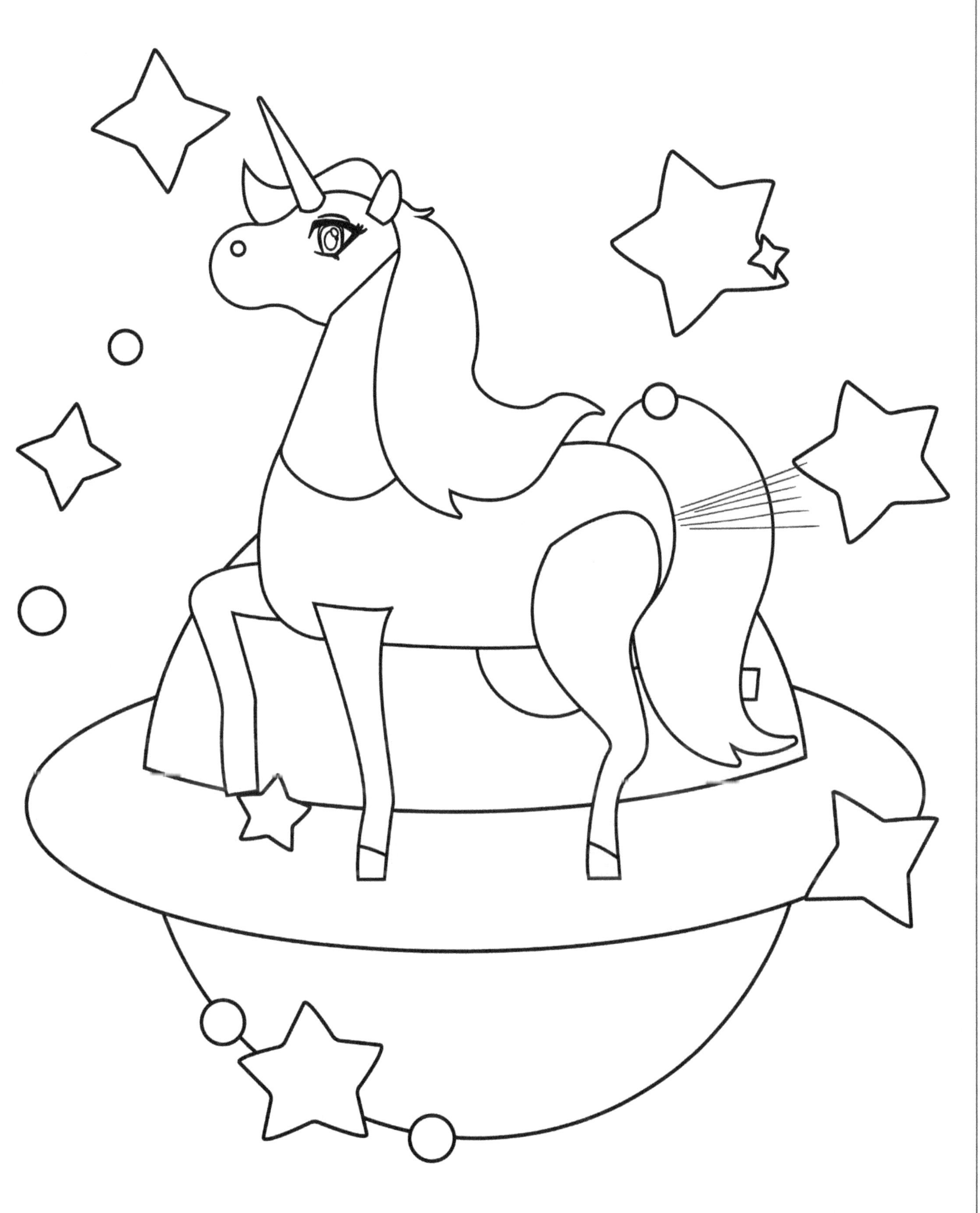

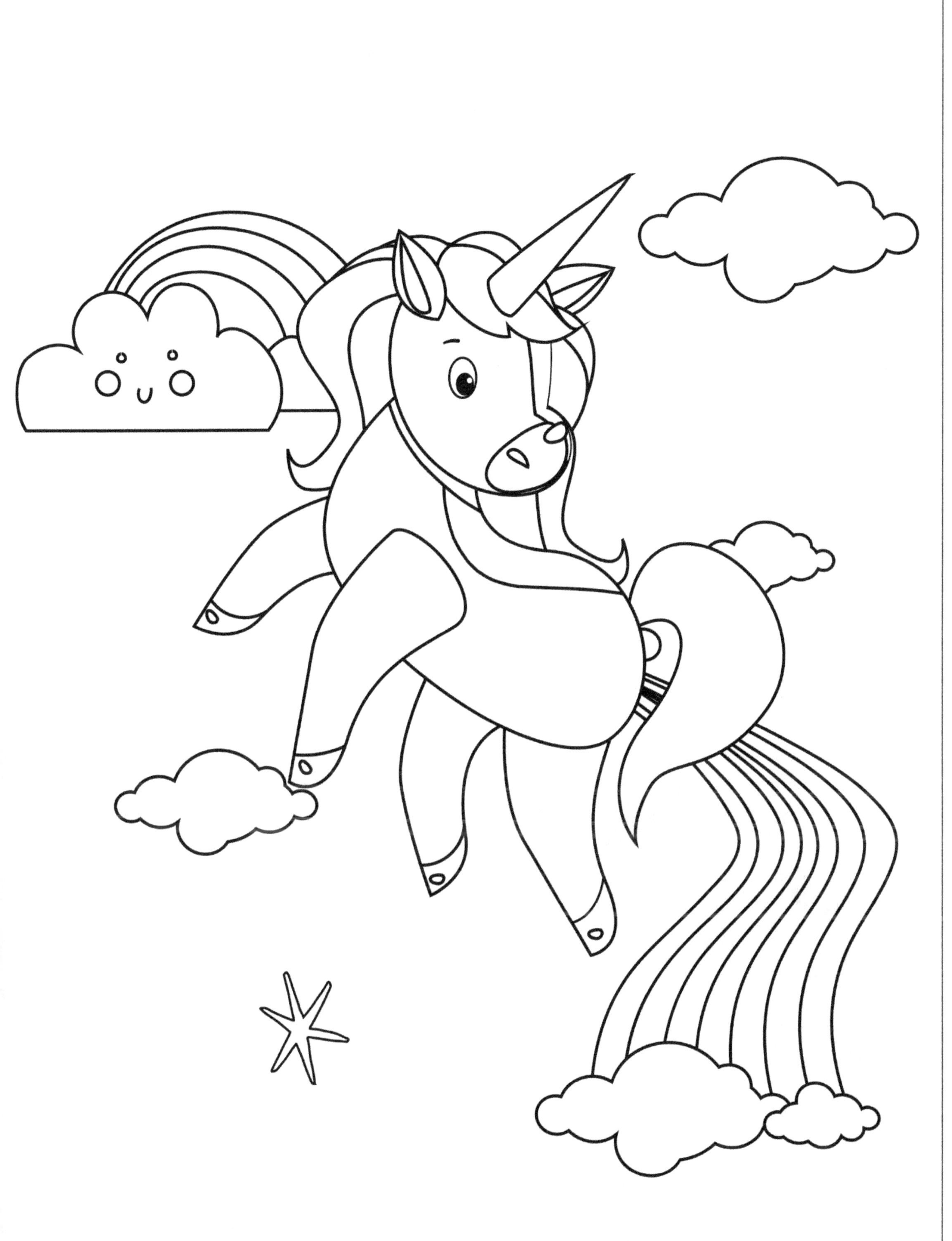

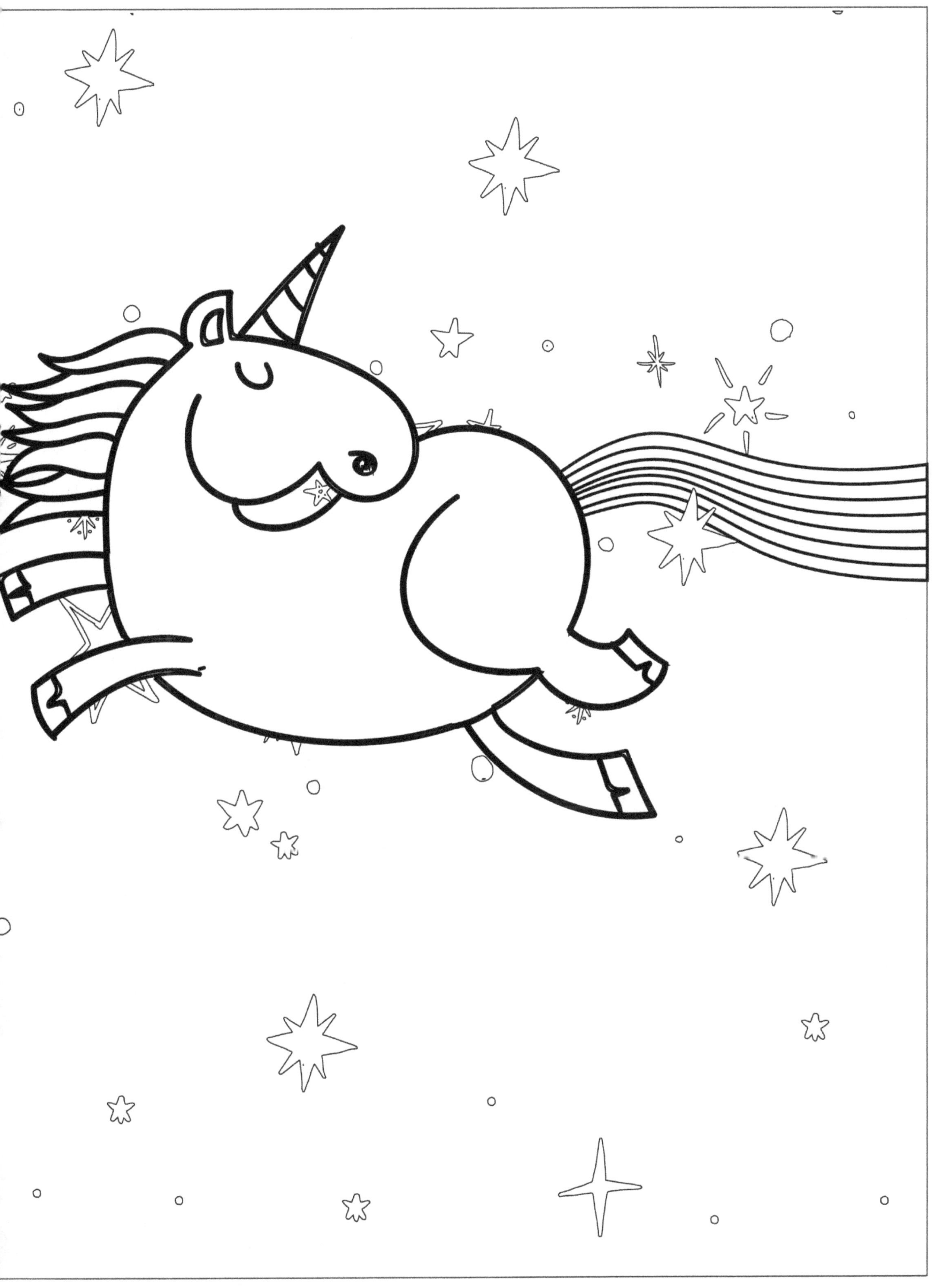

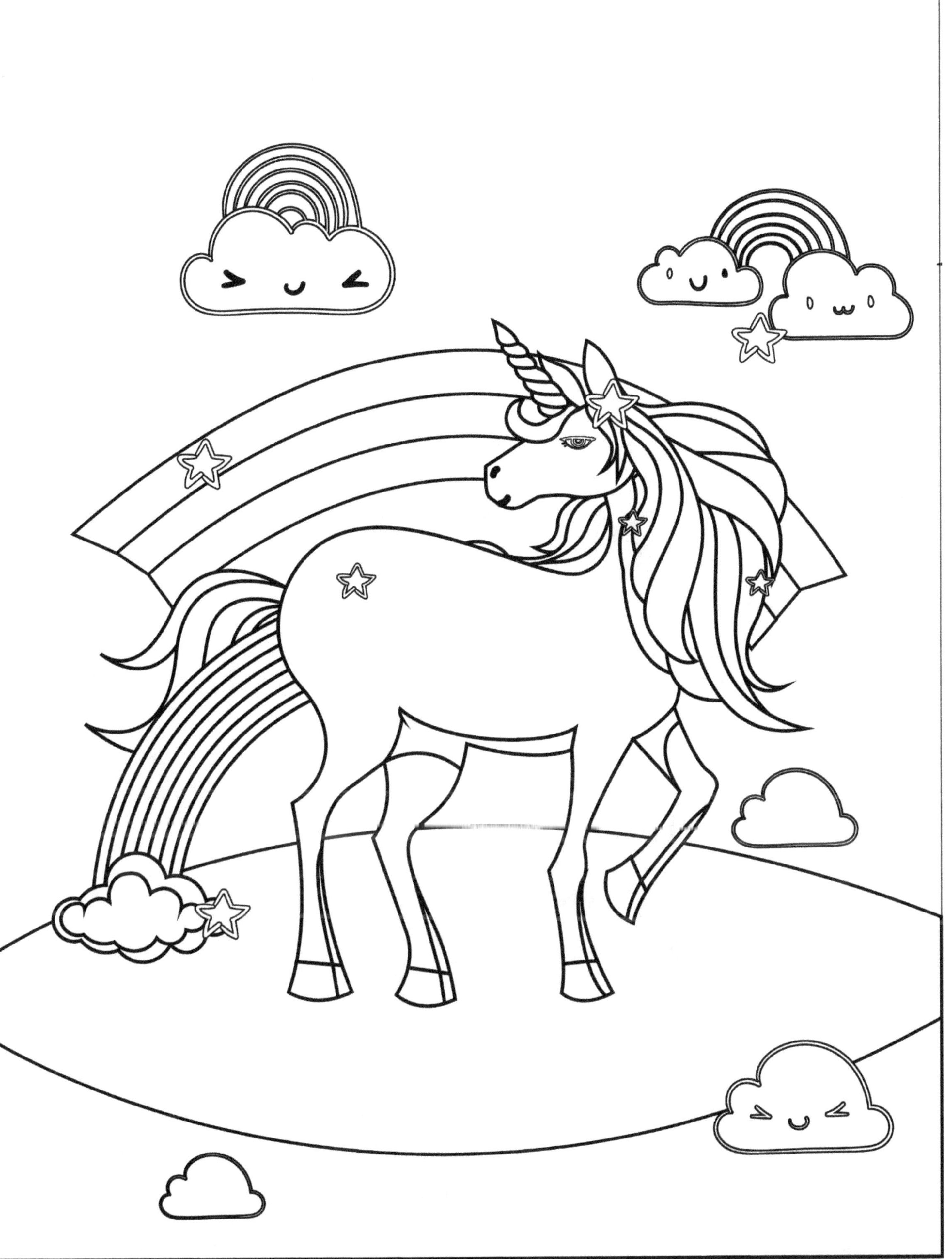

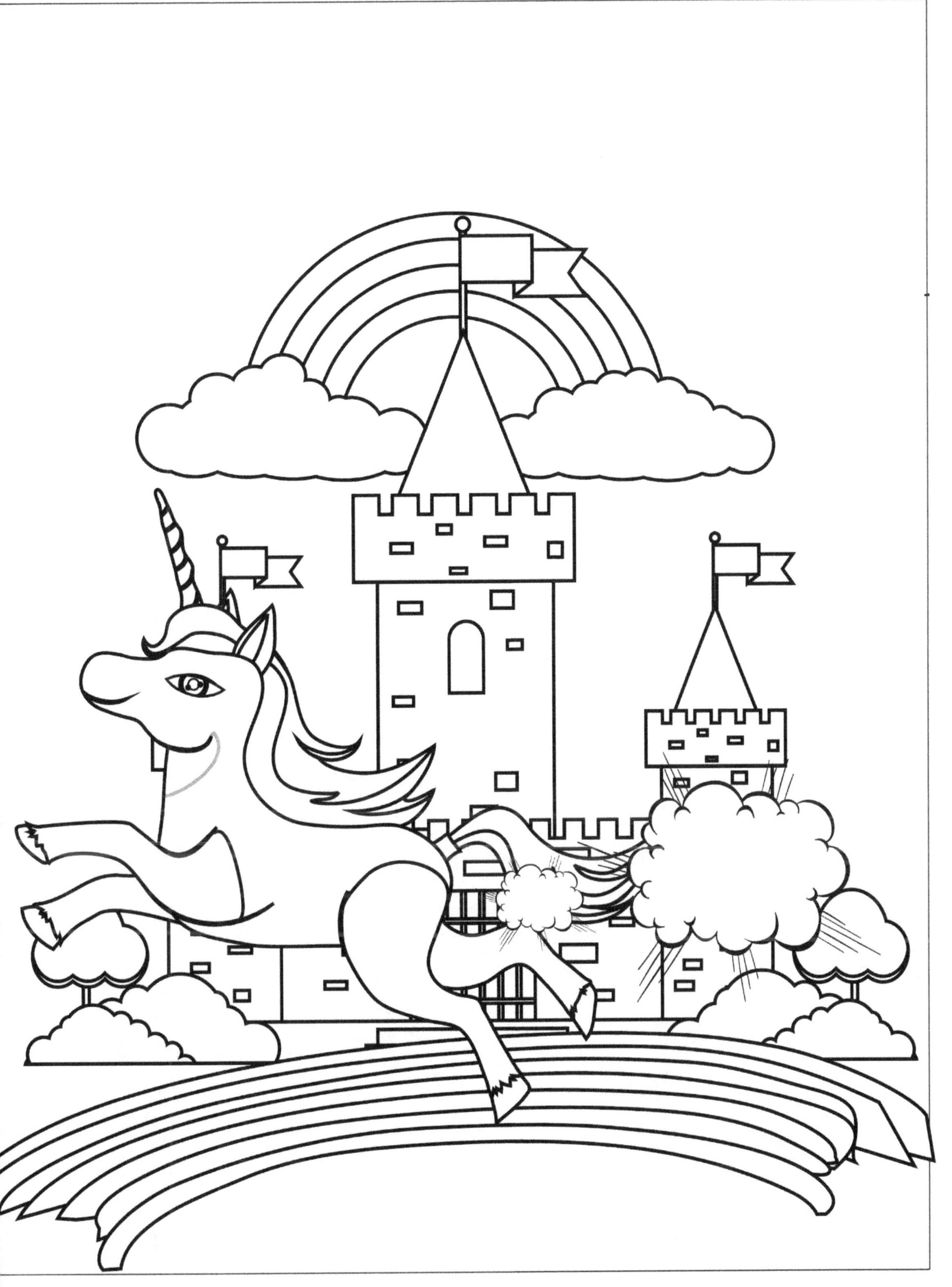

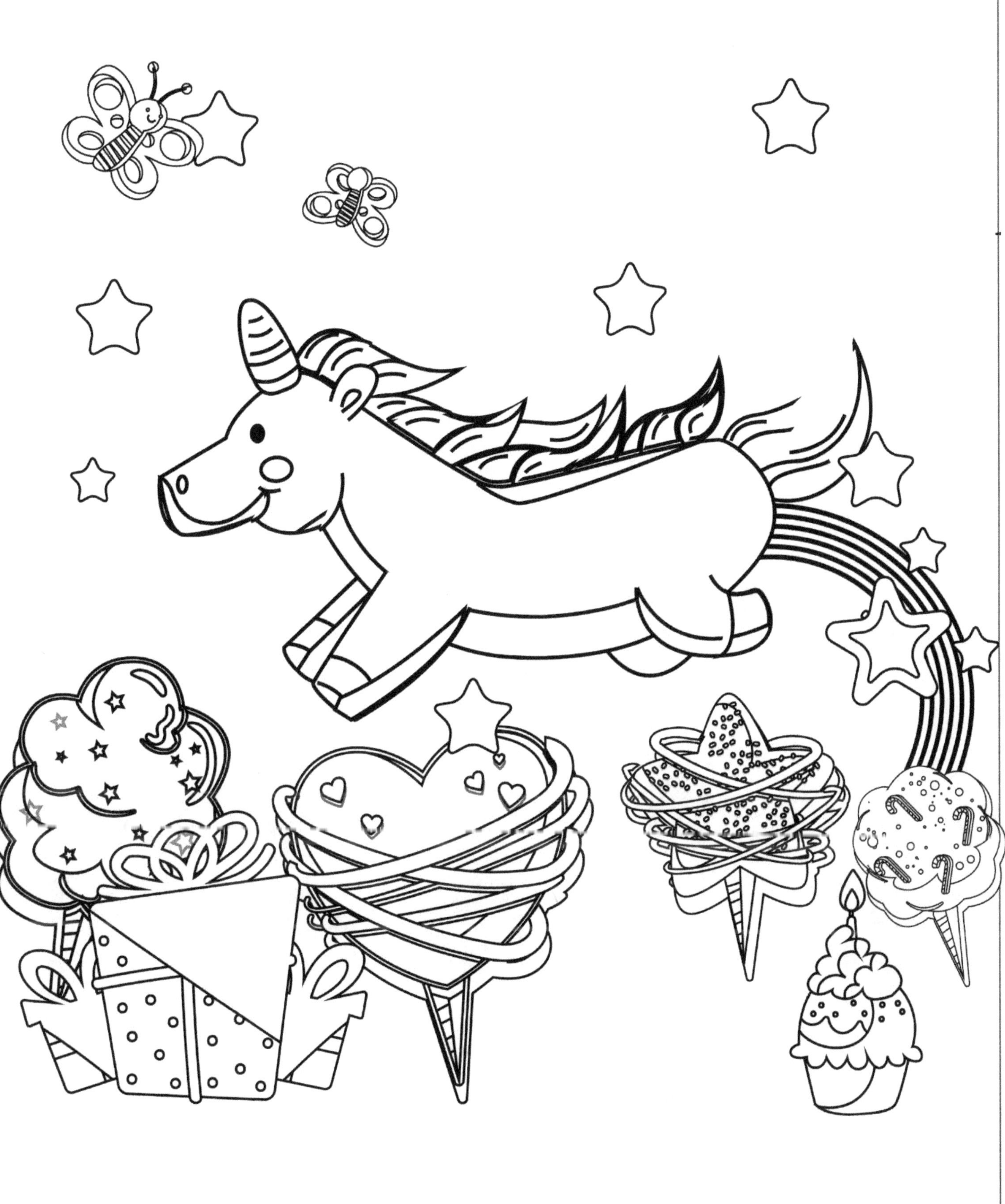

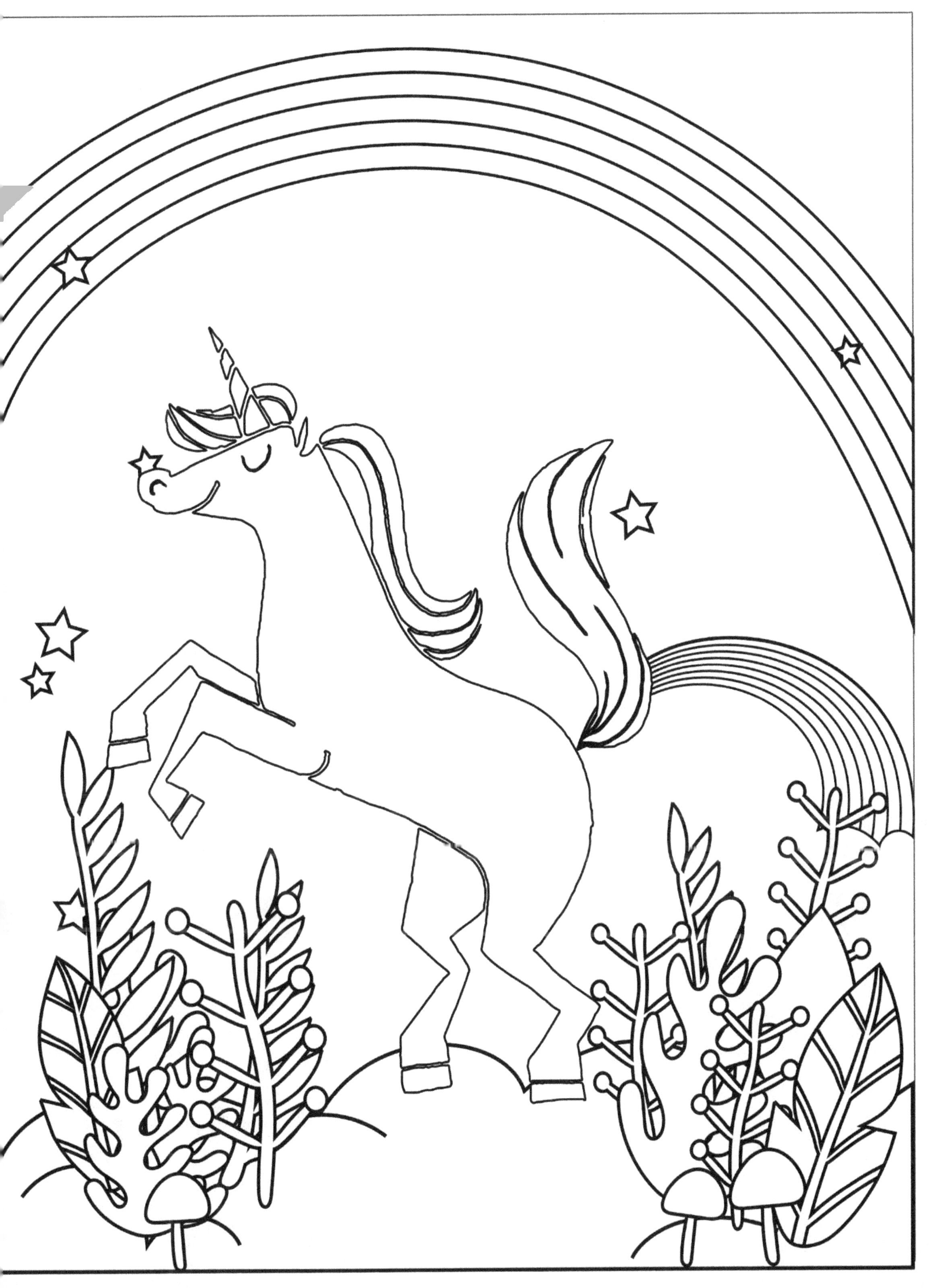

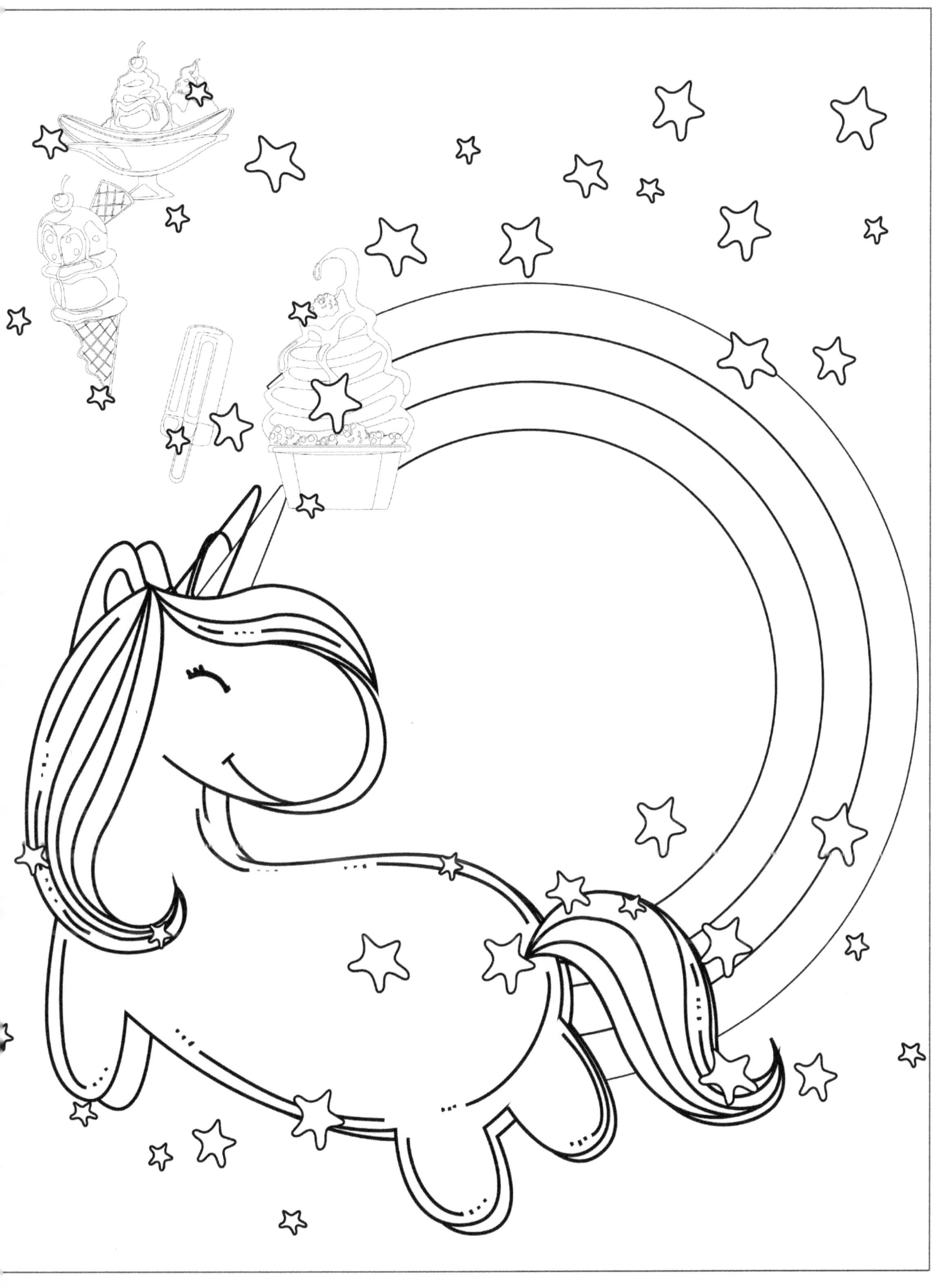

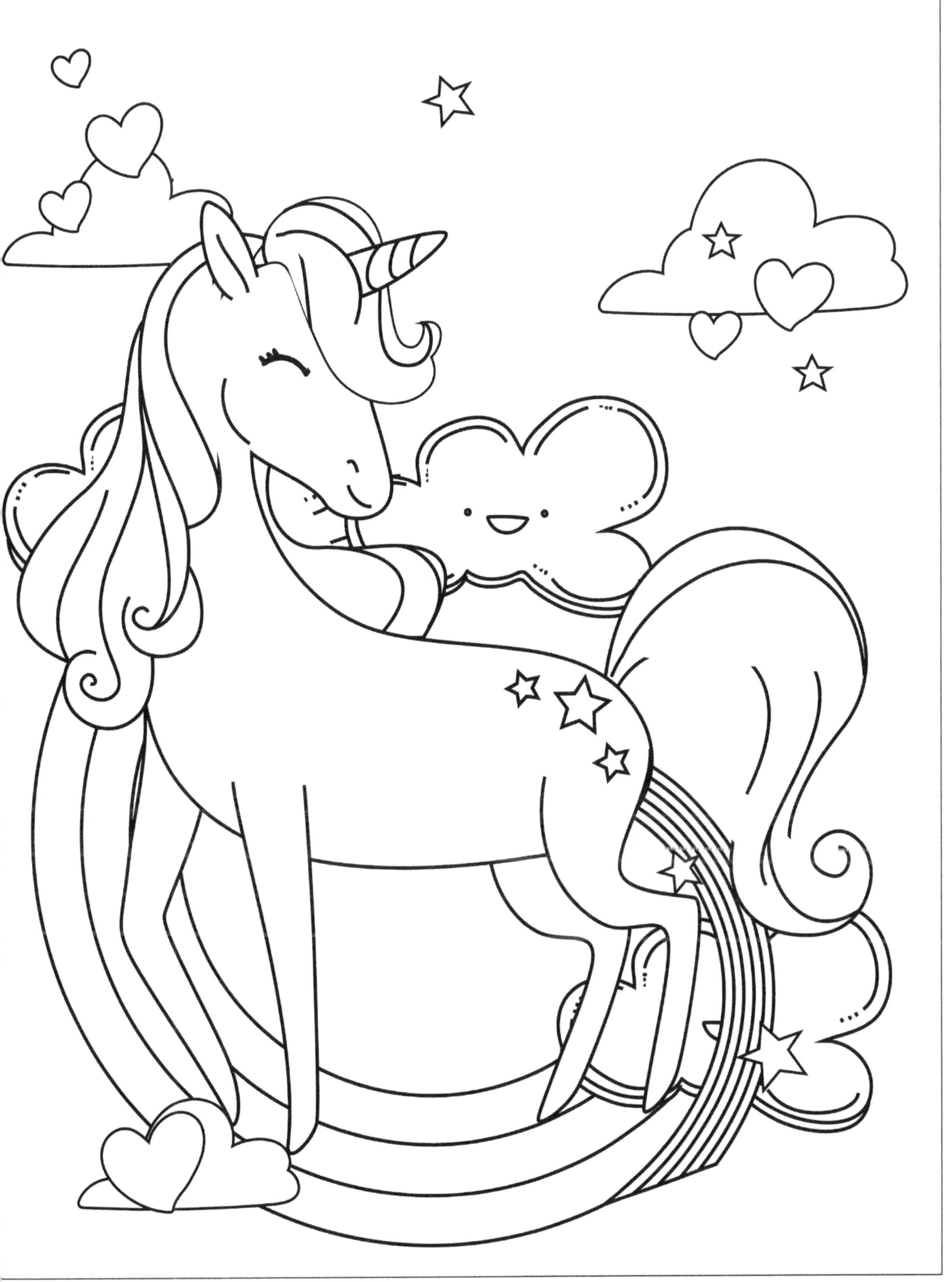

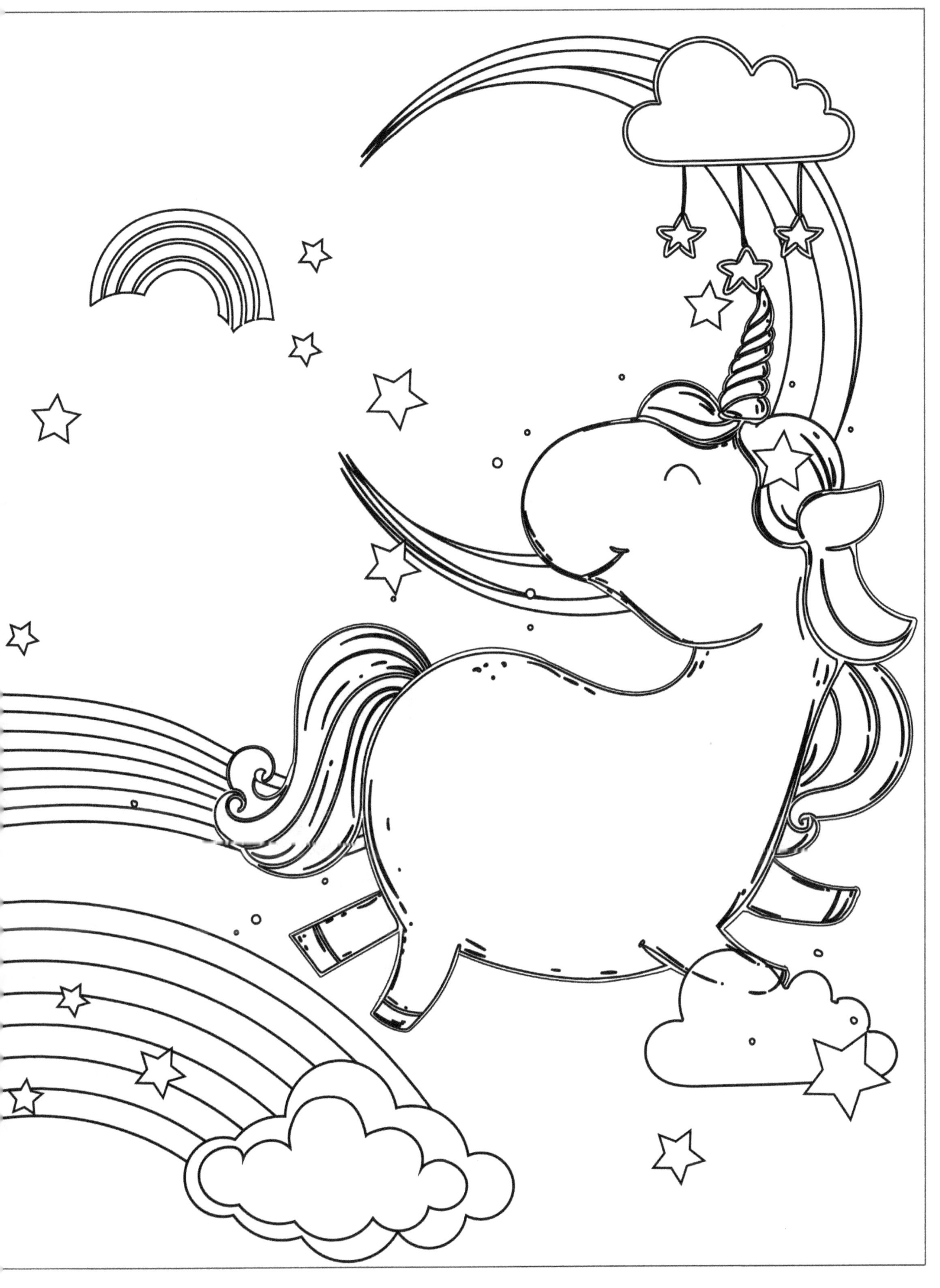

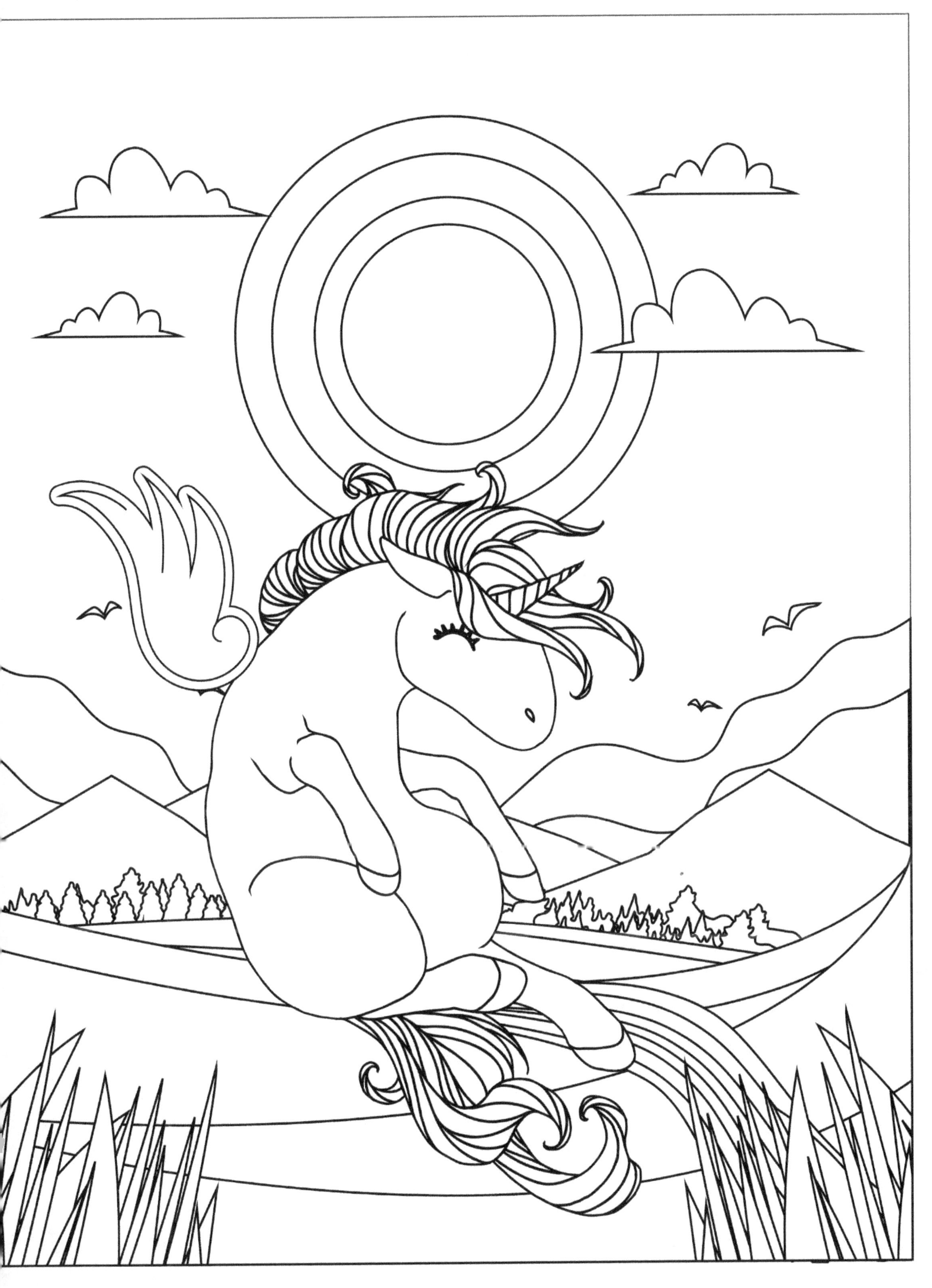

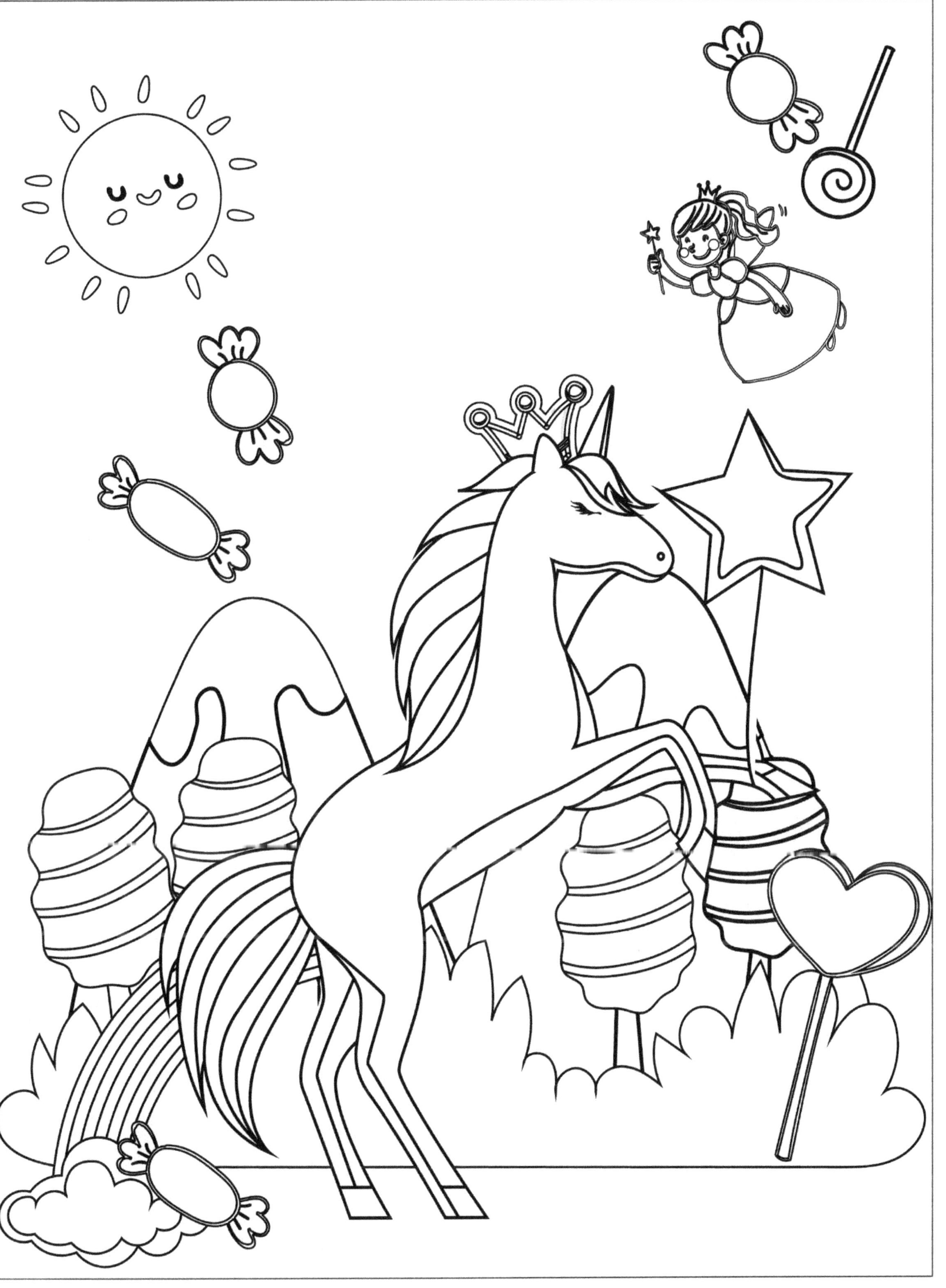

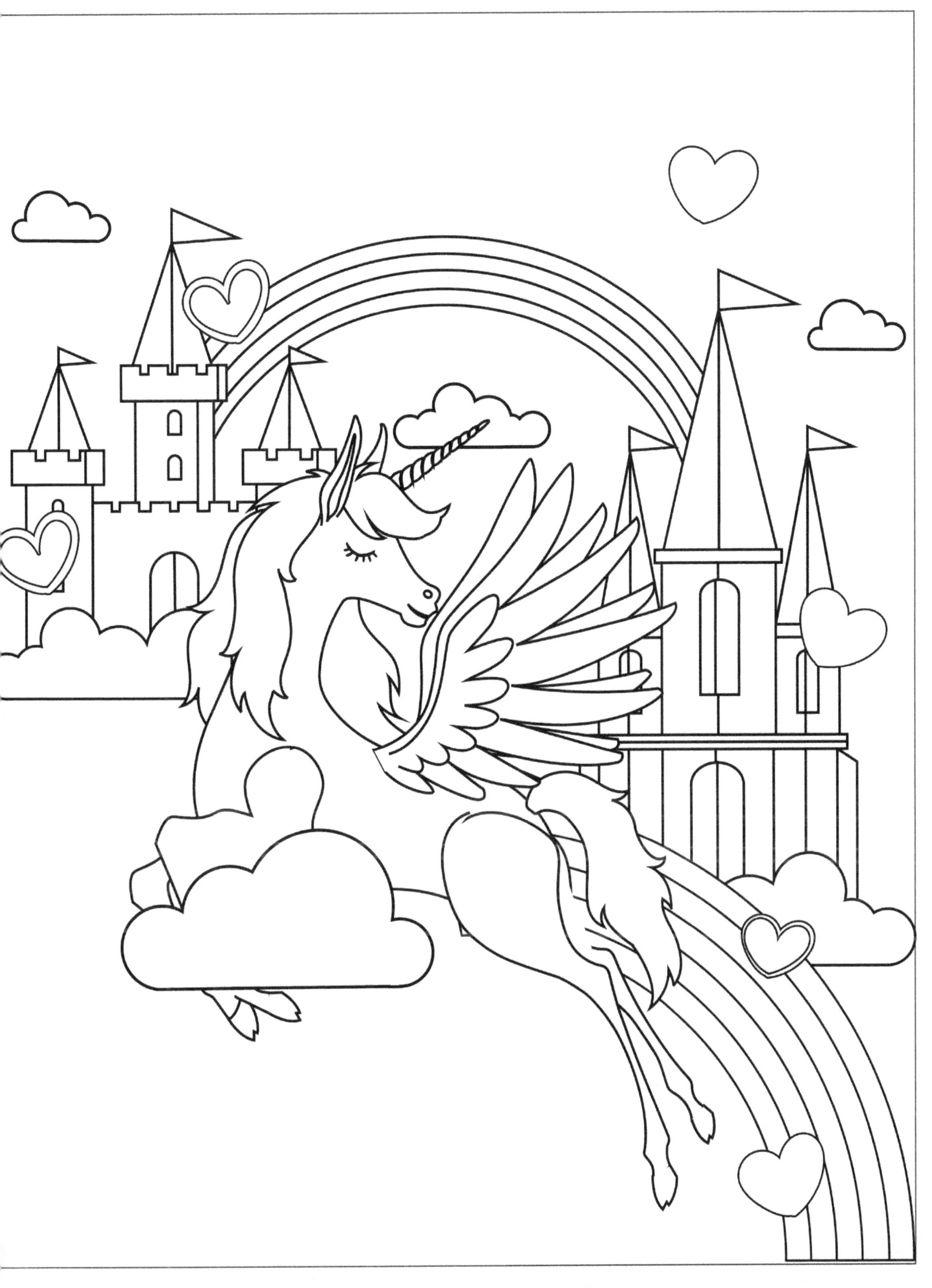

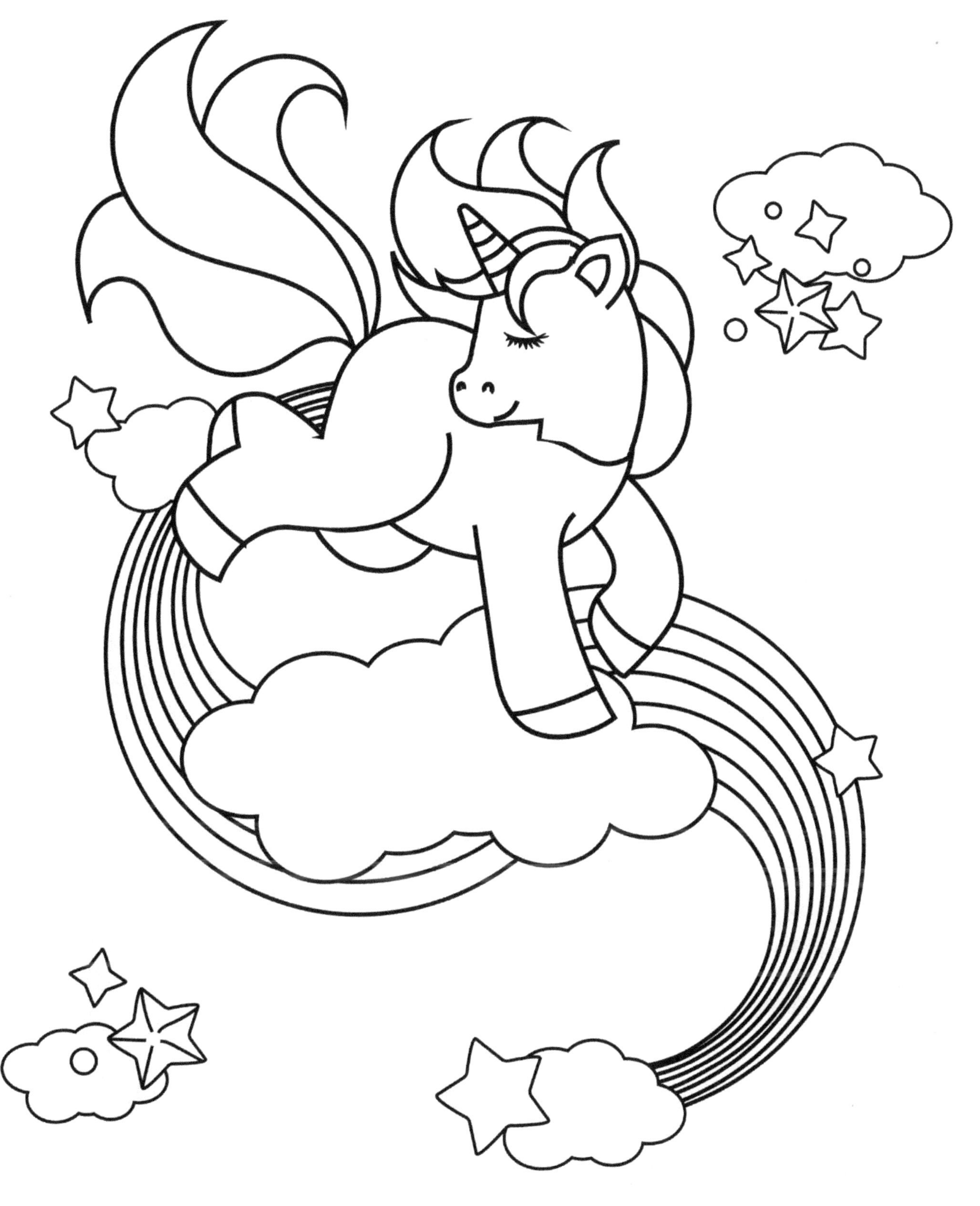

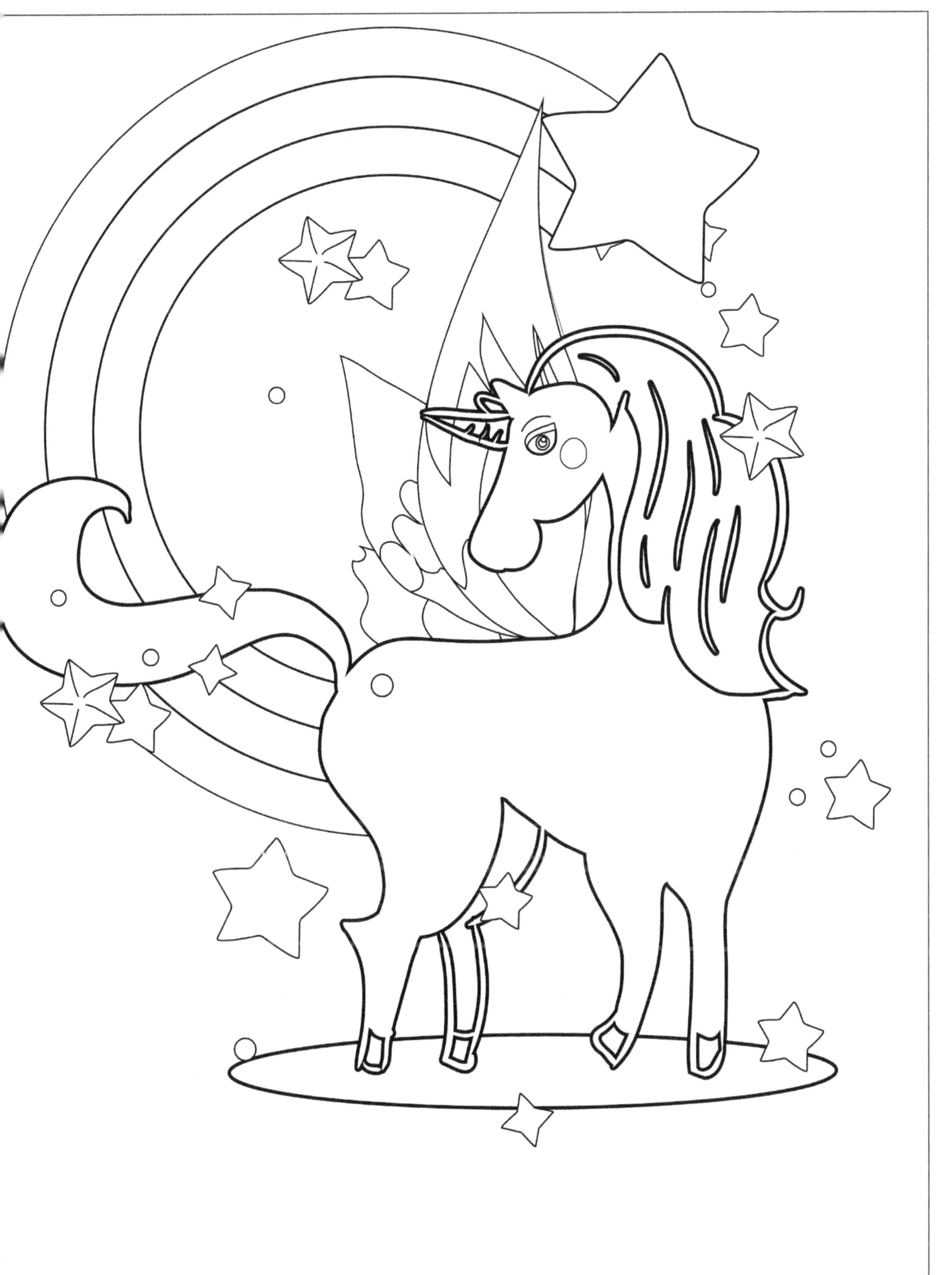

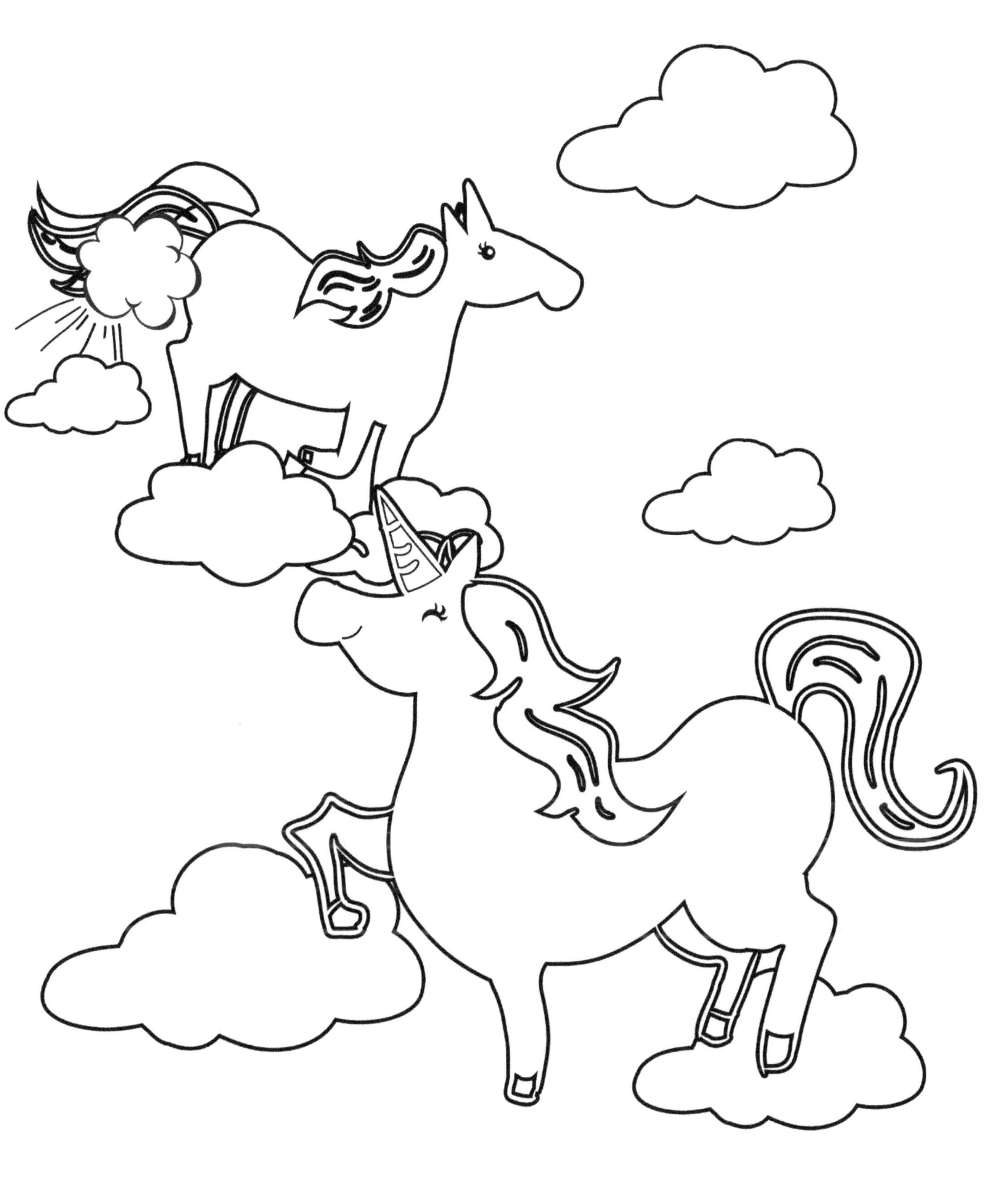

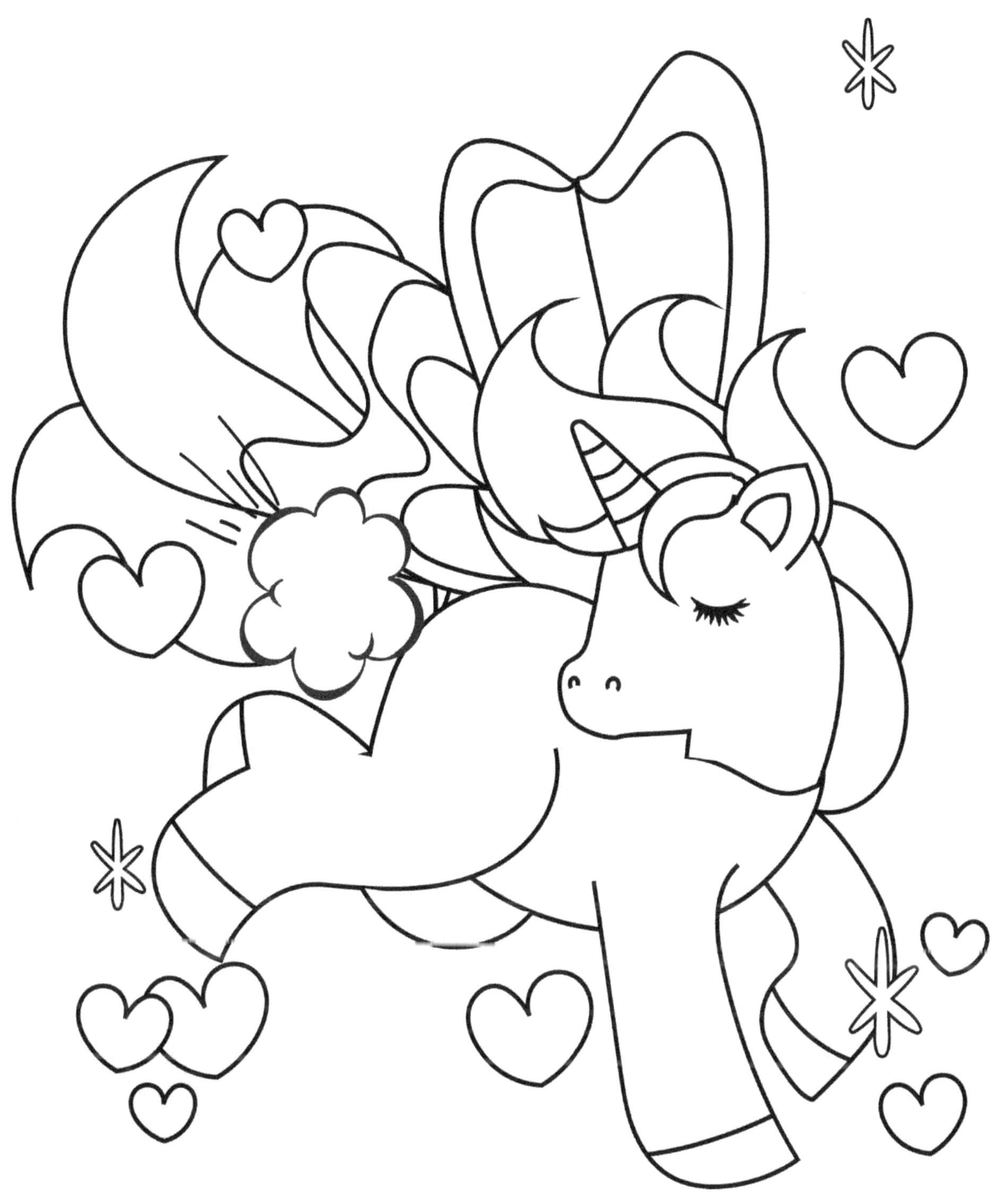

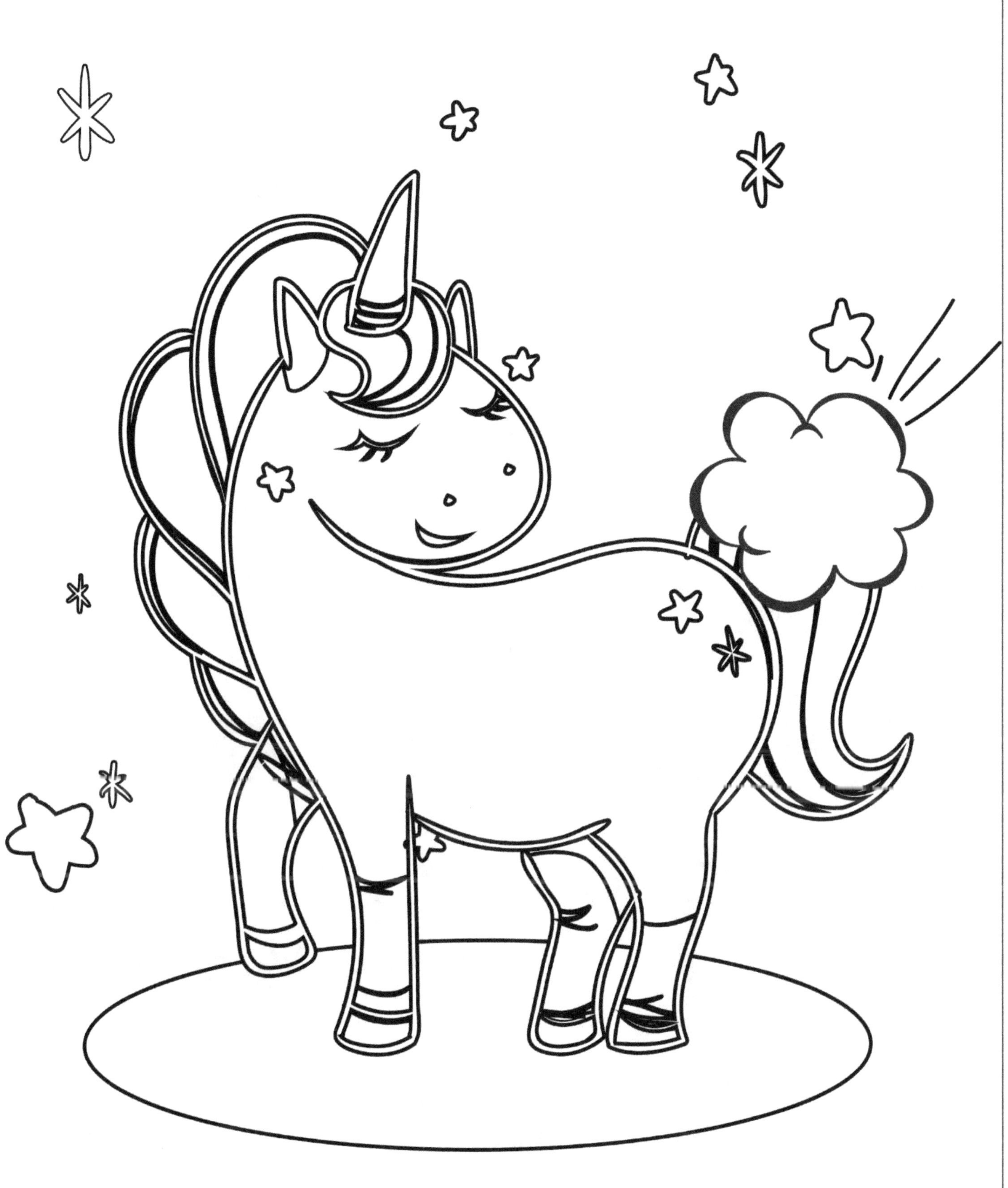

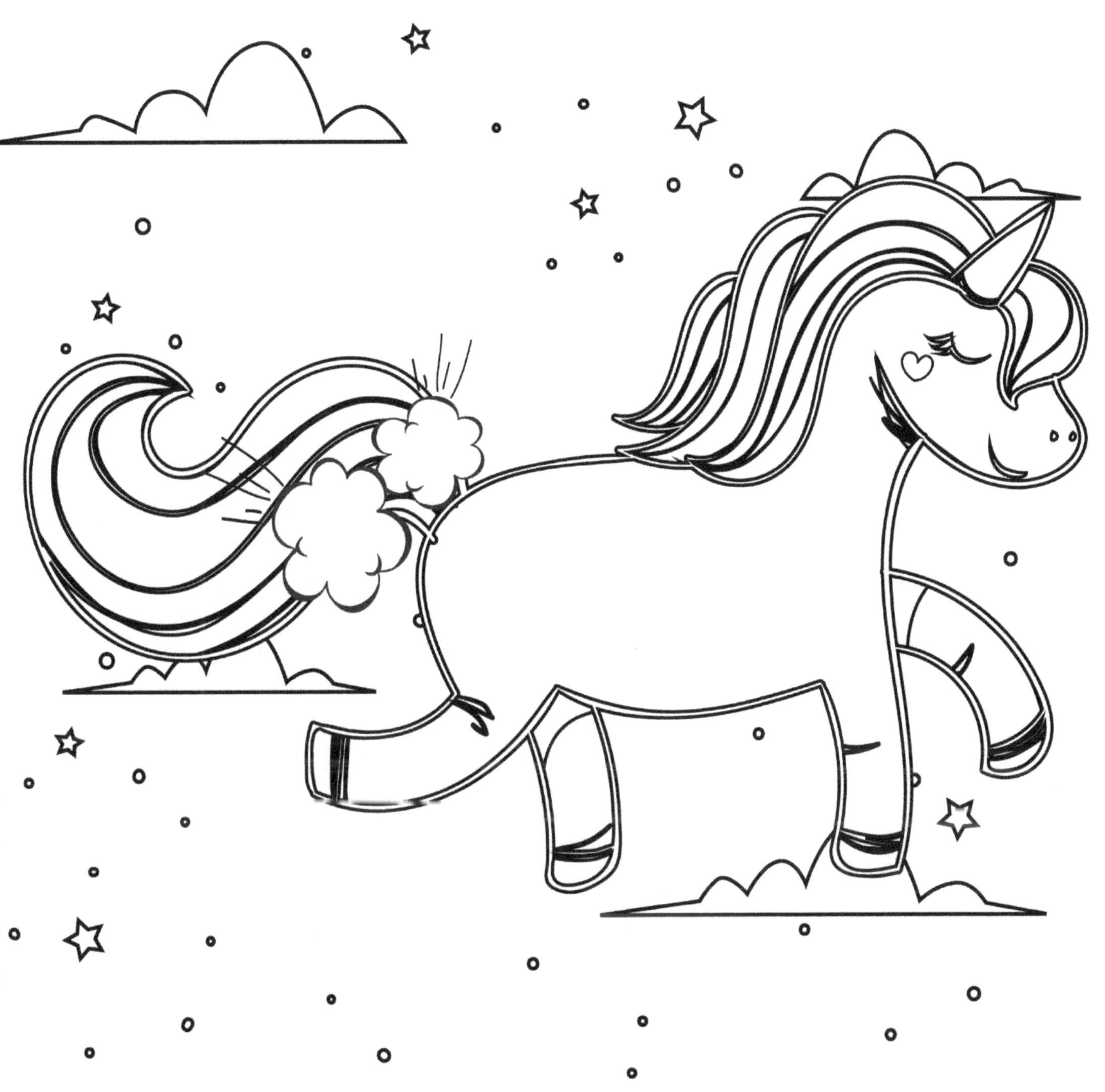

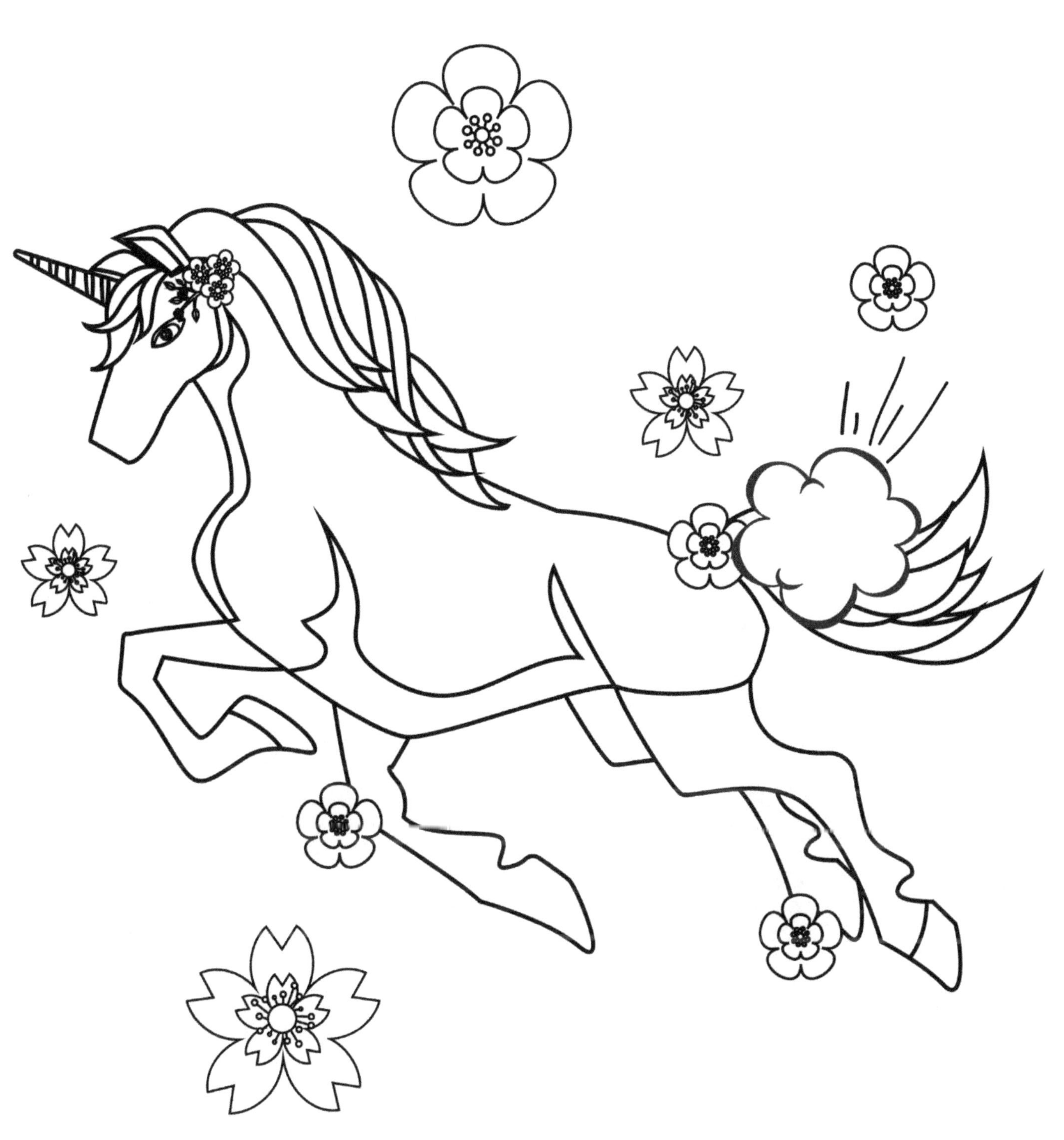

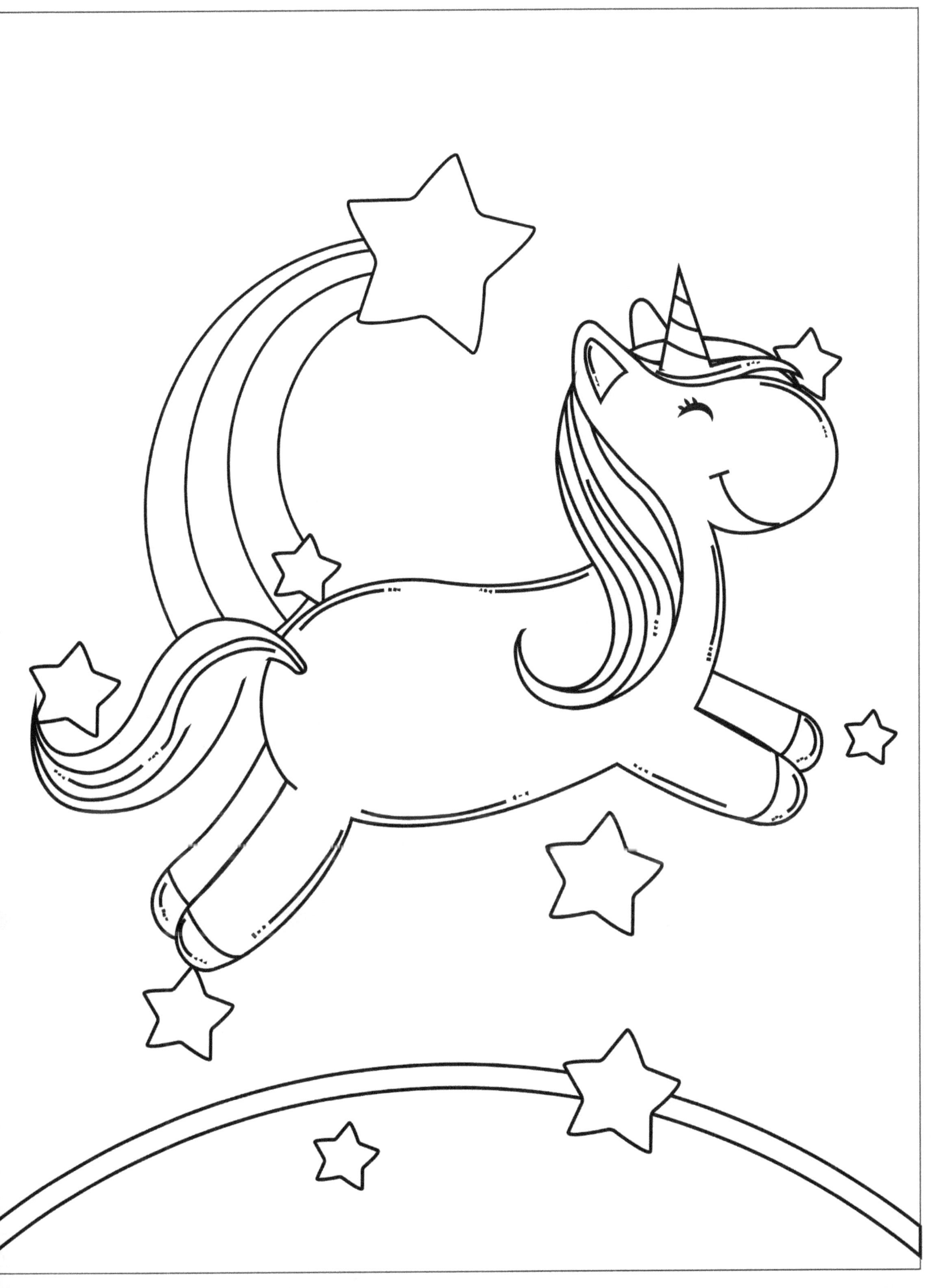

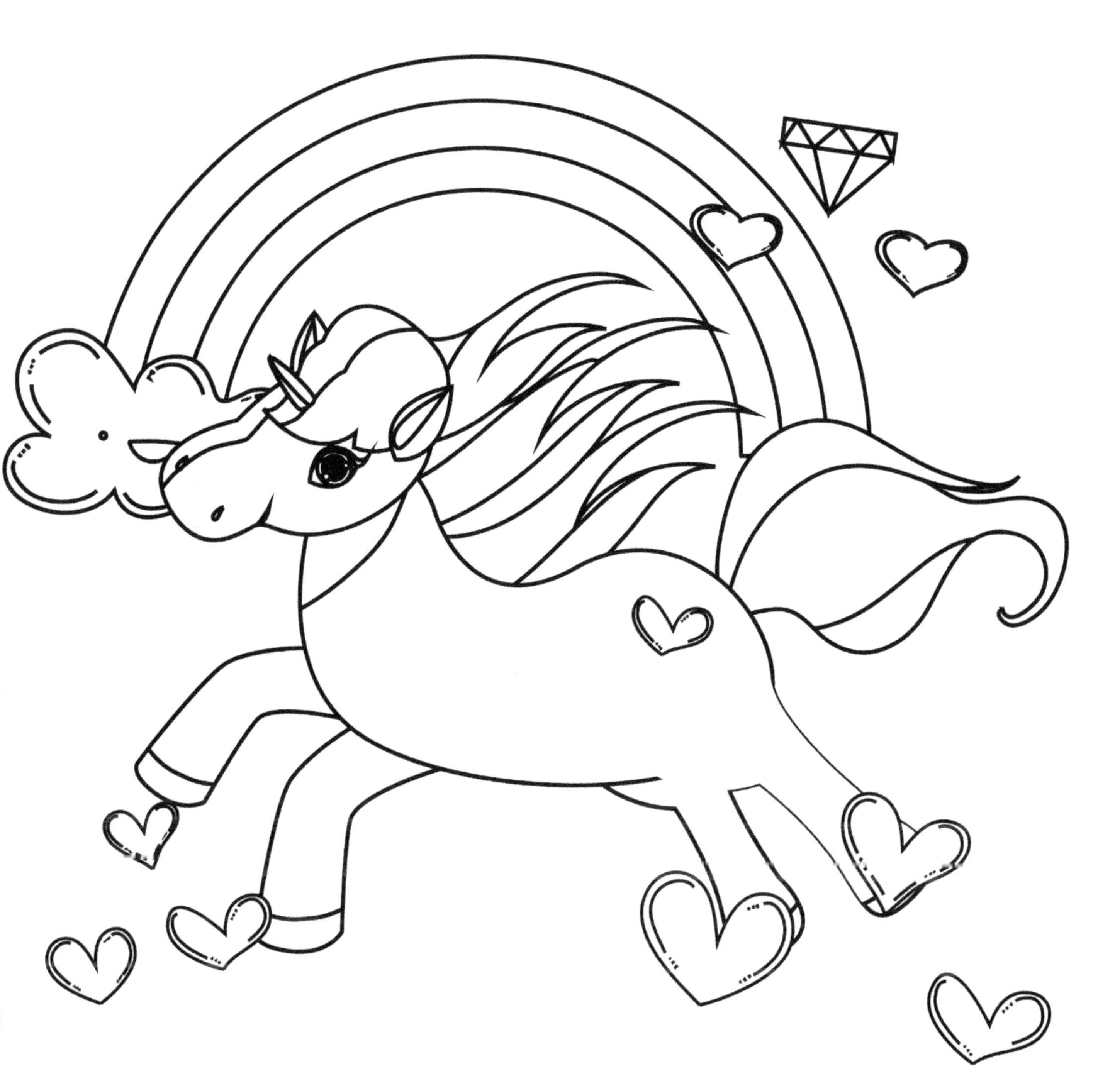

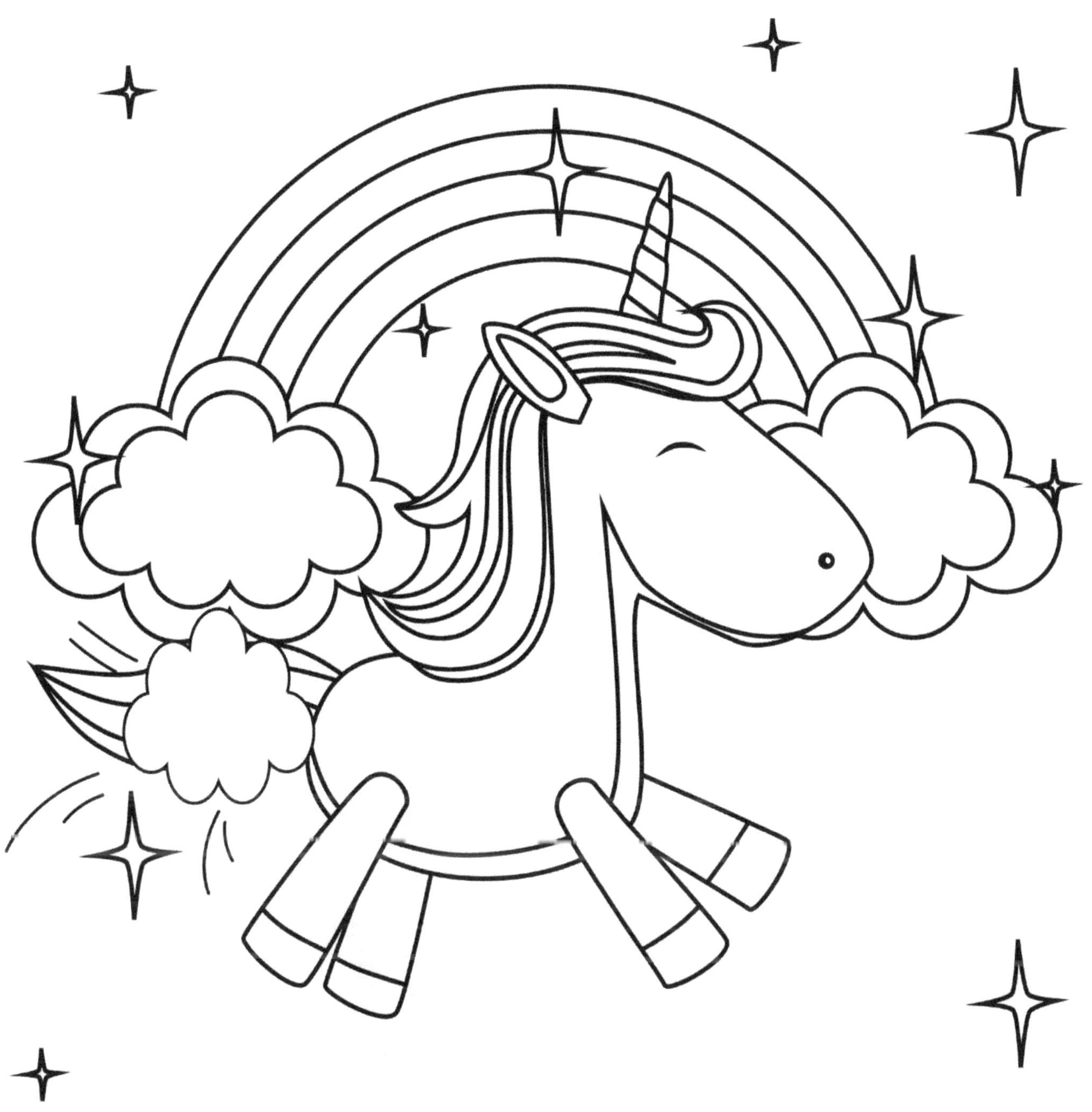

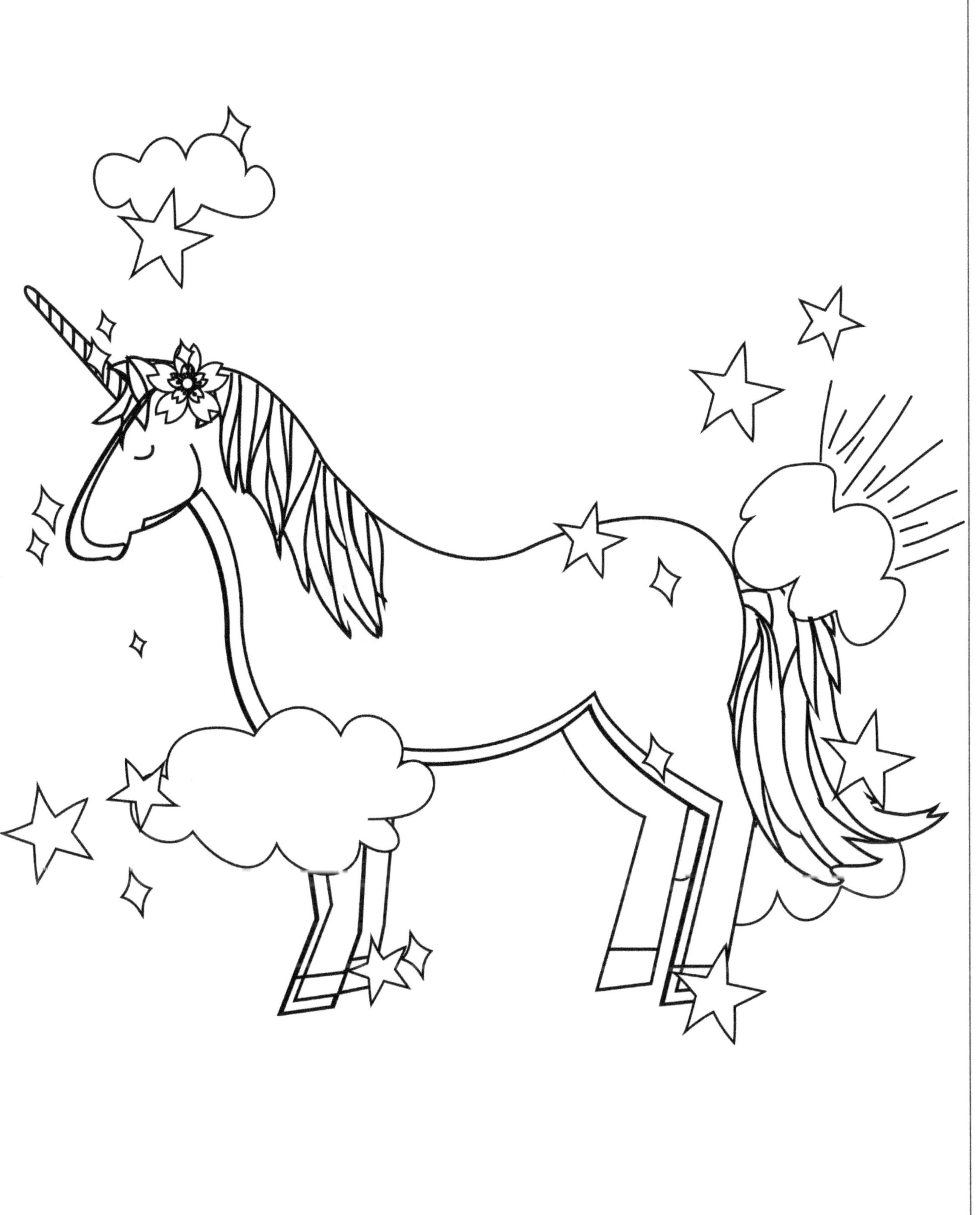

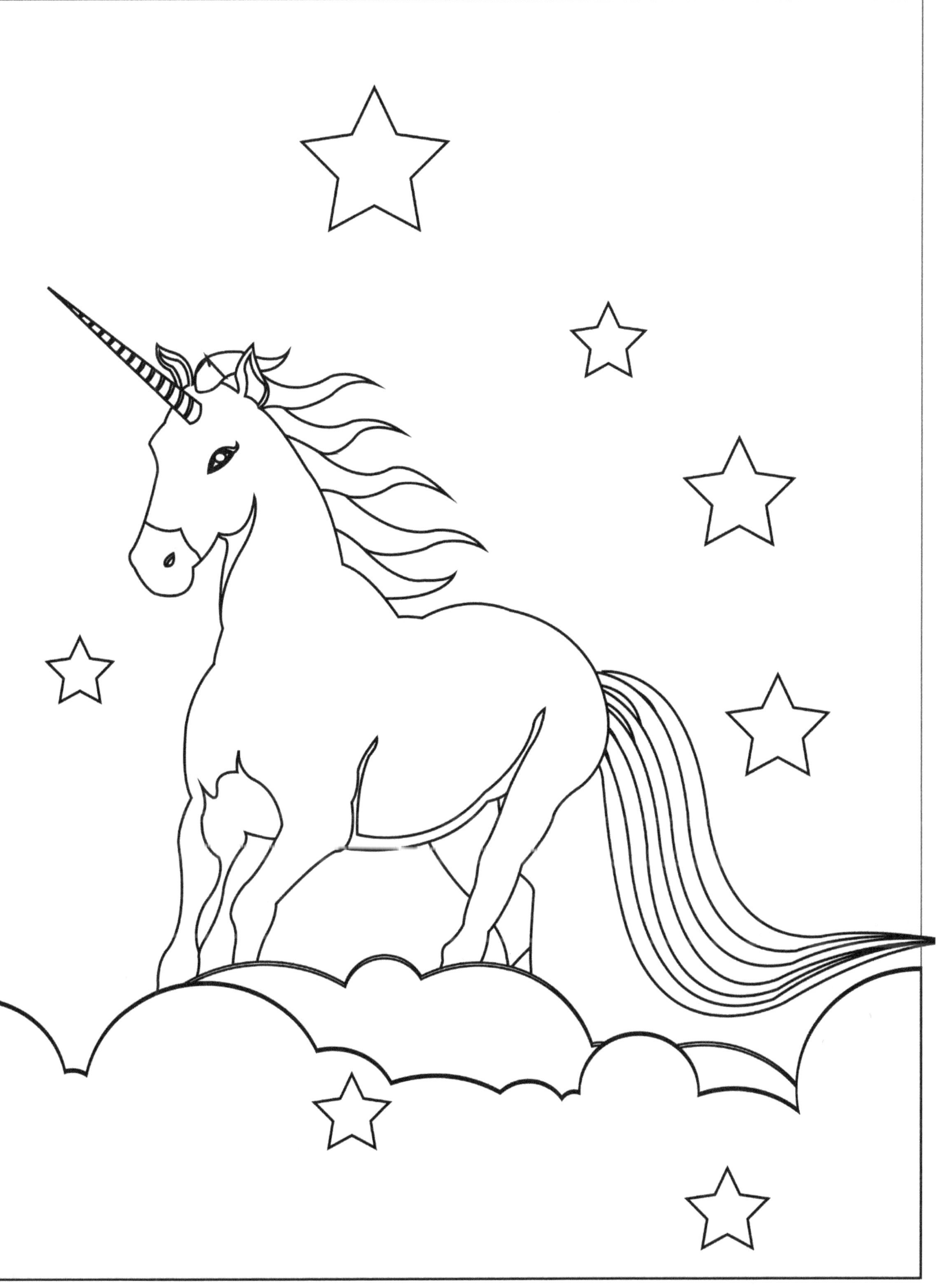

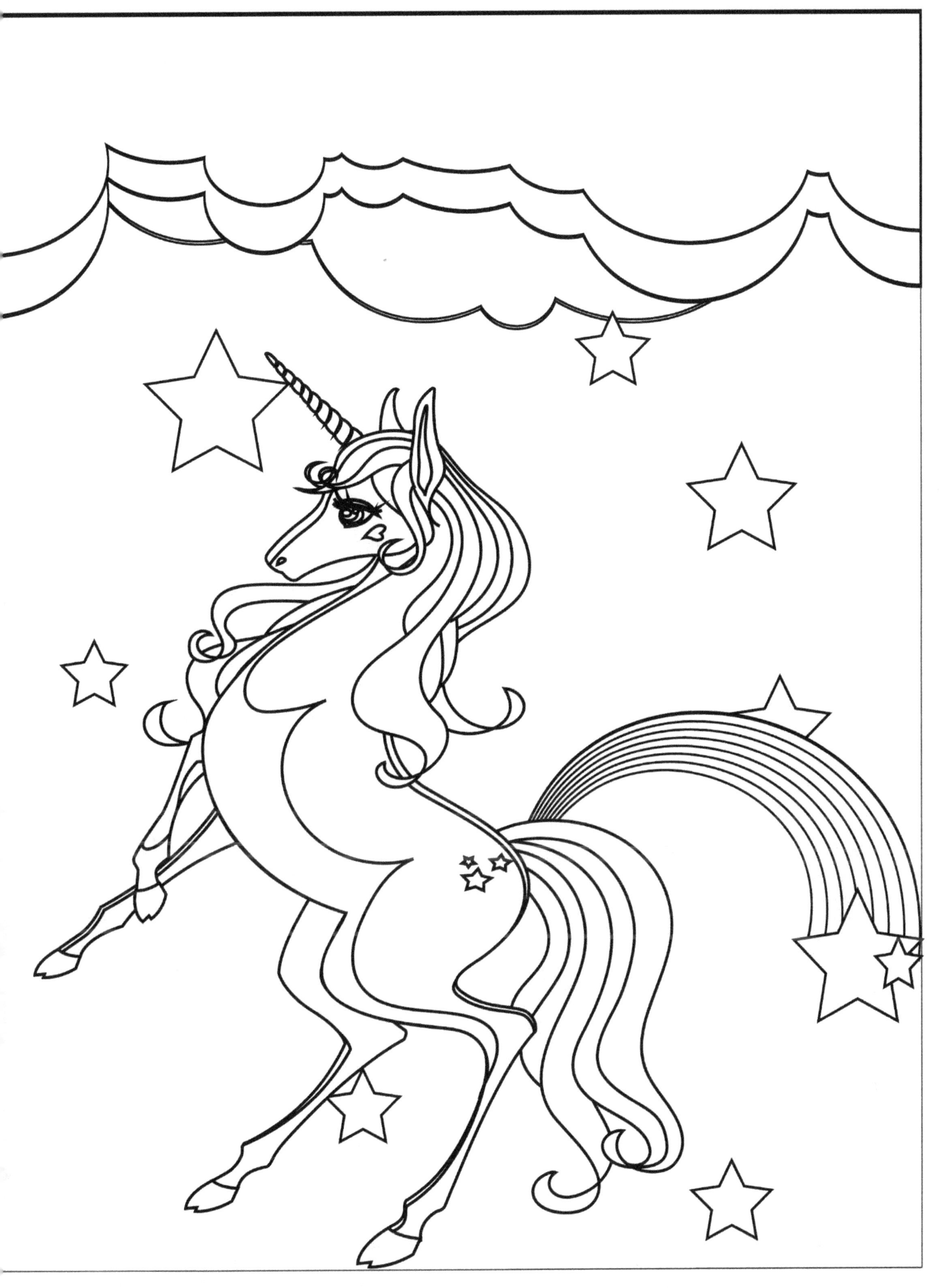

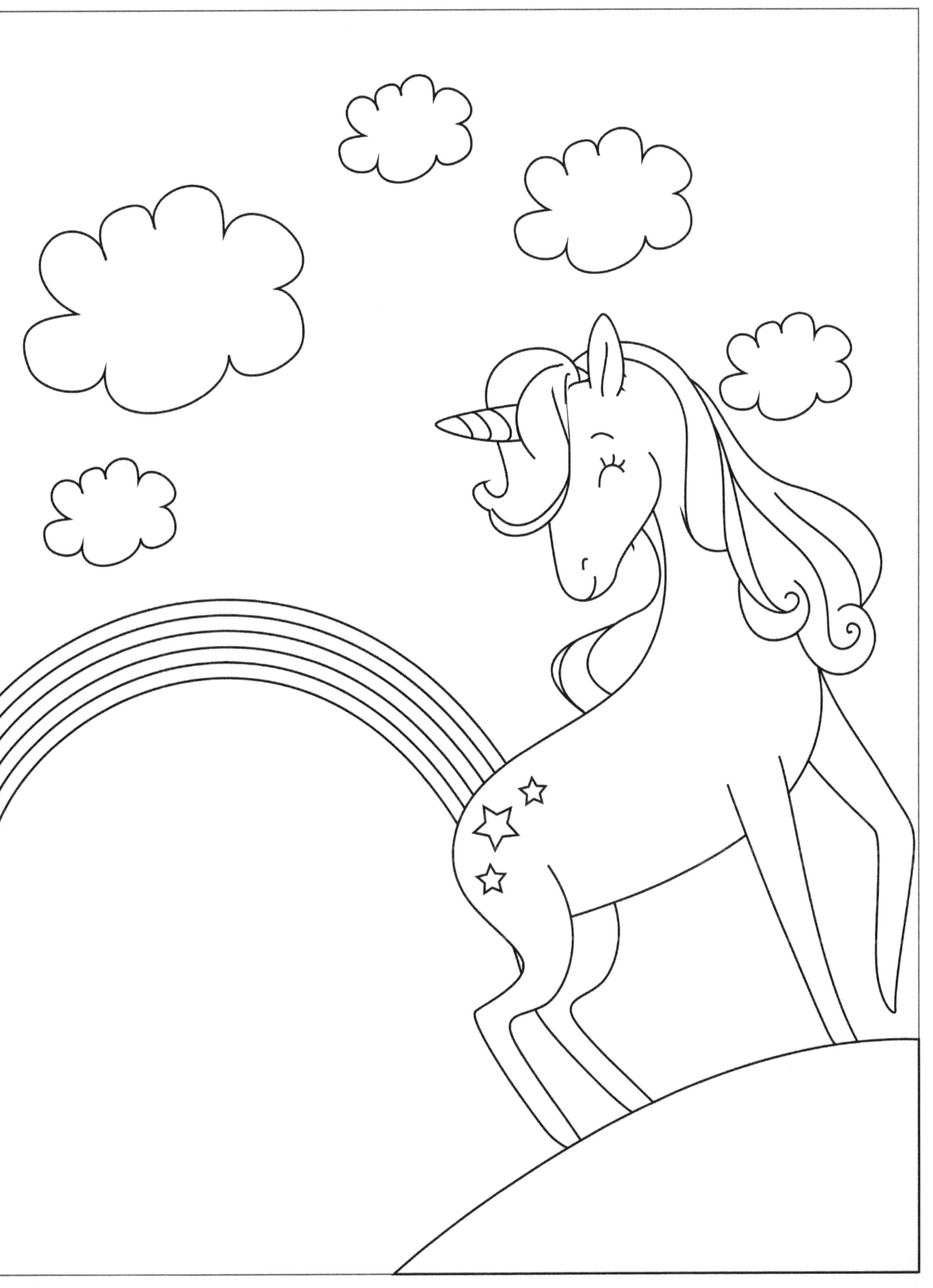

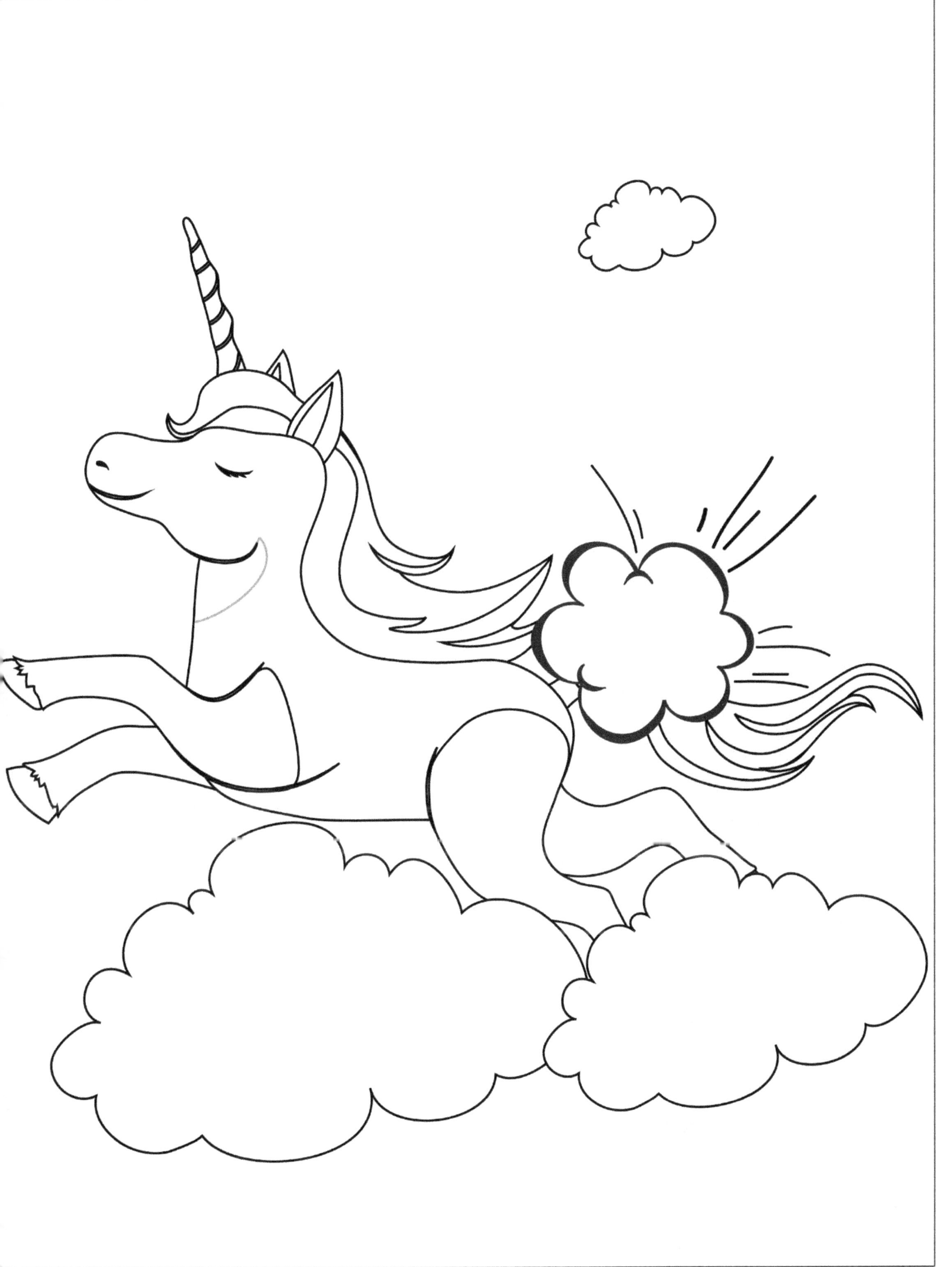

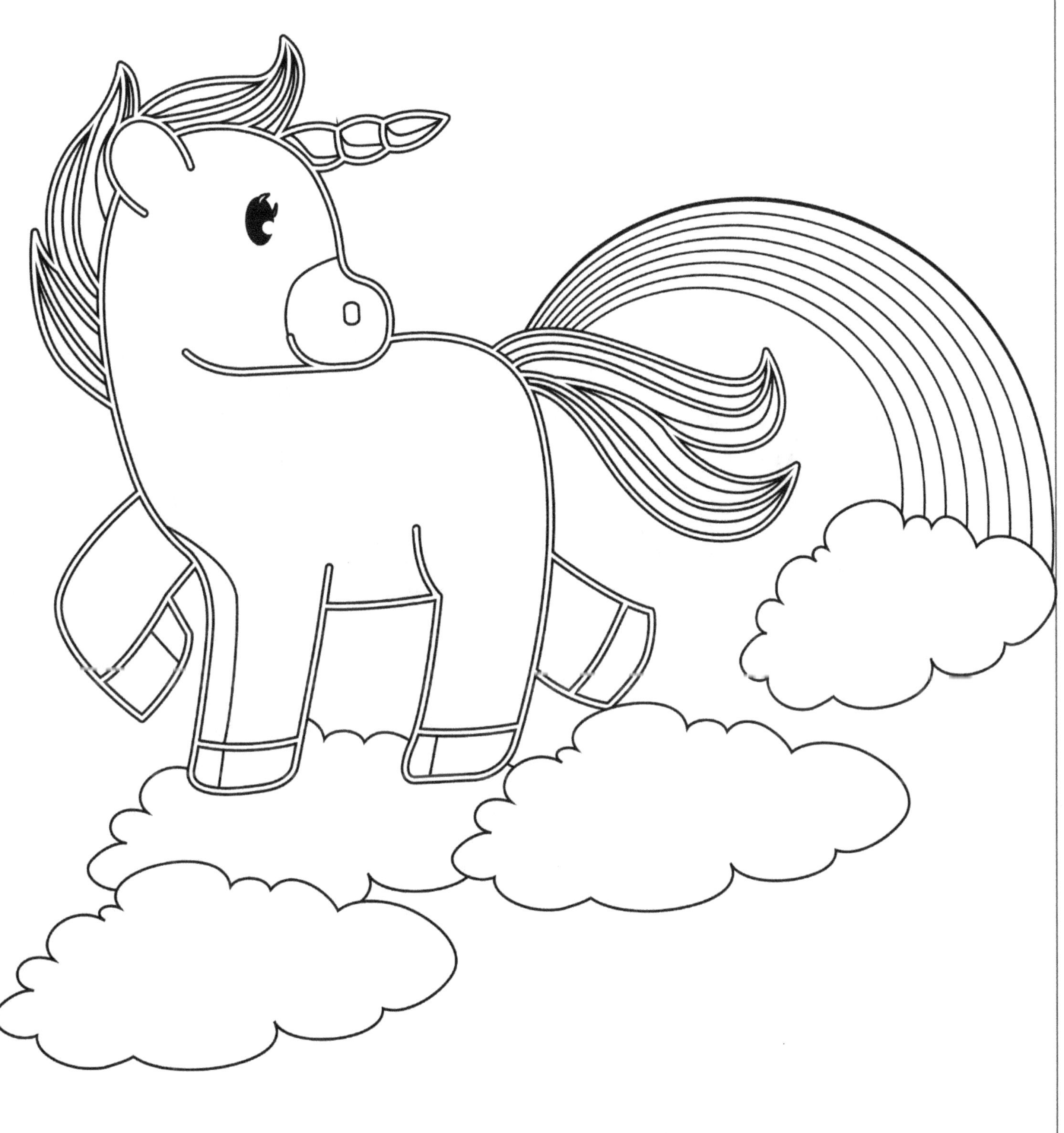

Bonus

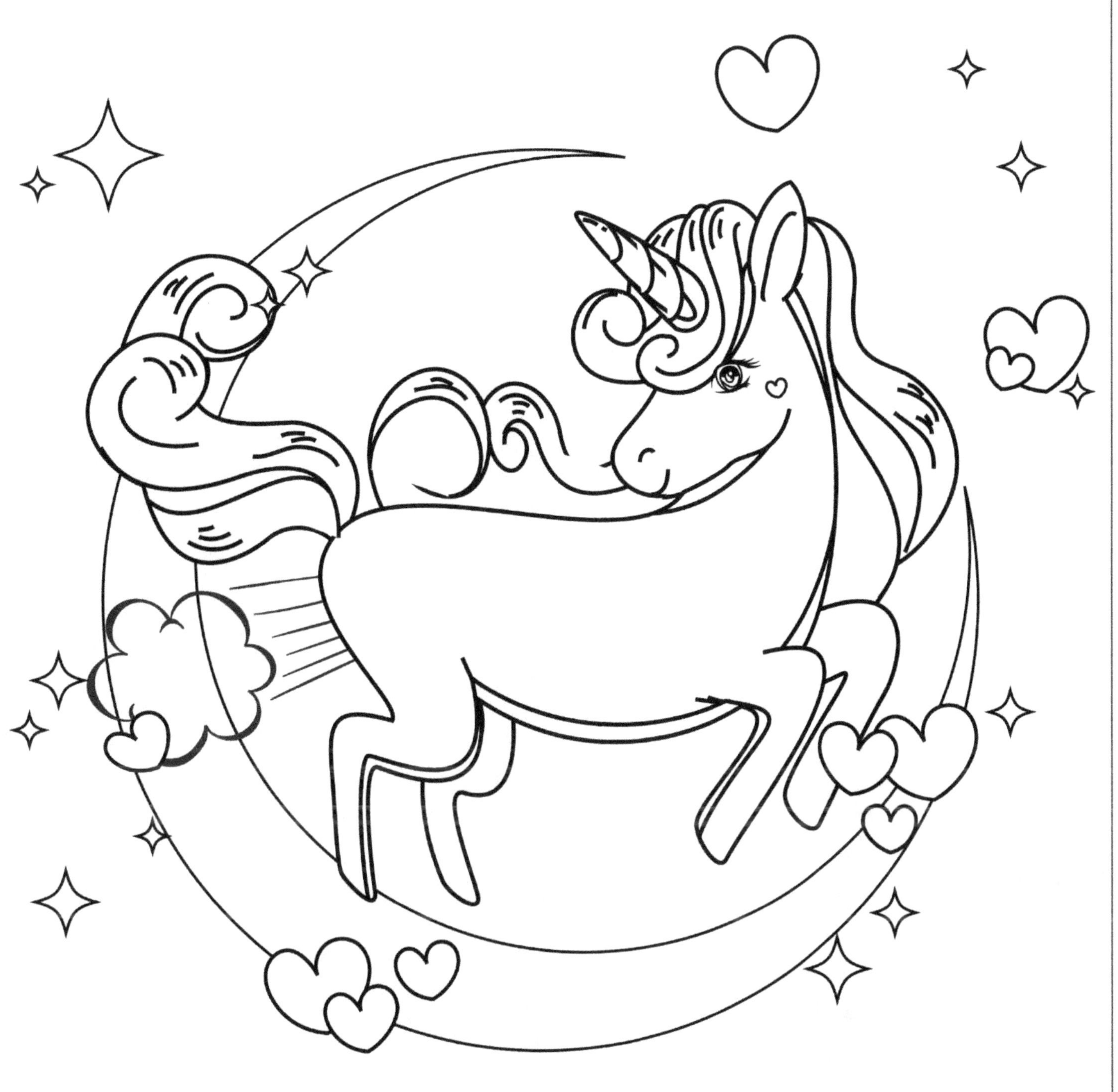

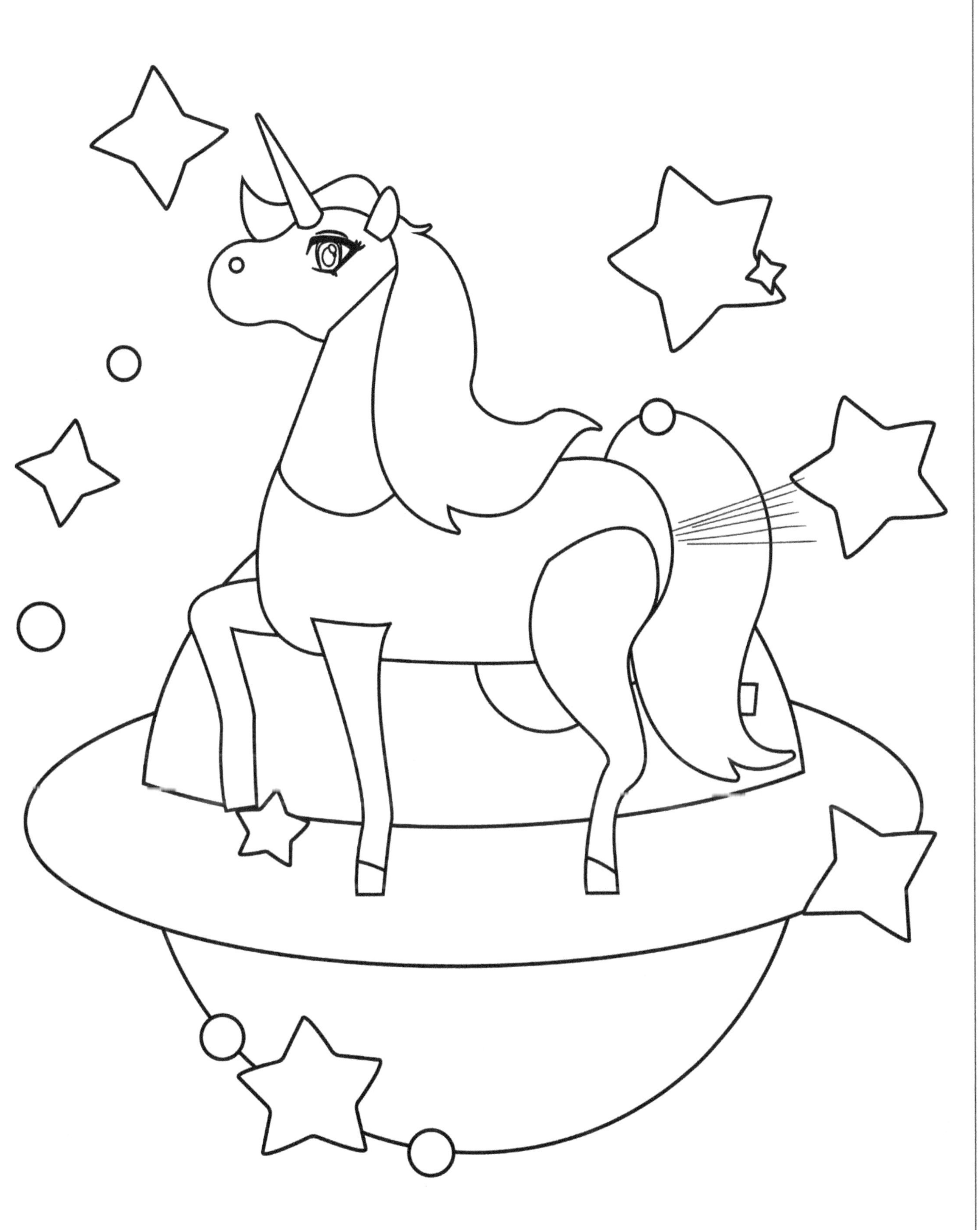

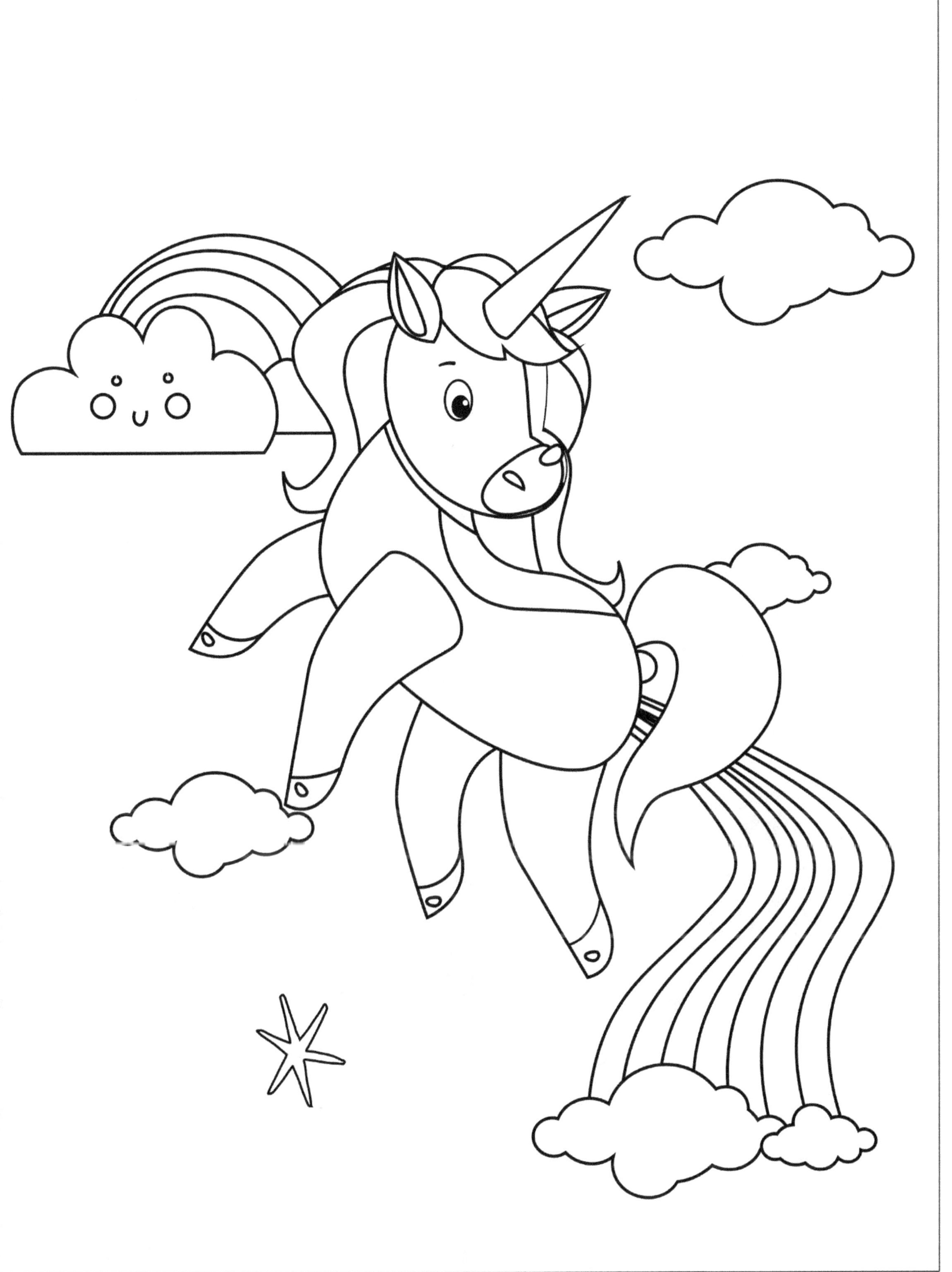

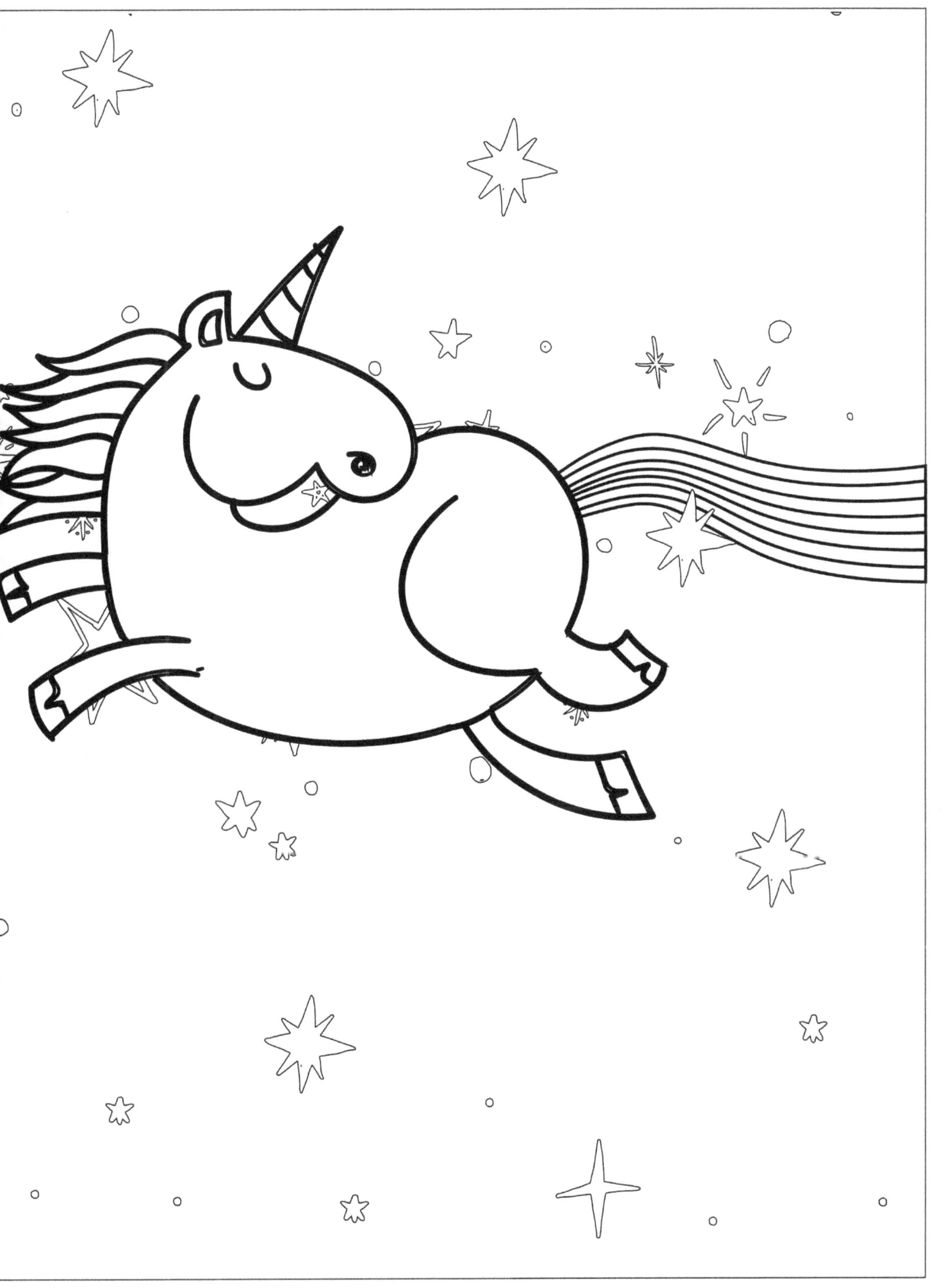

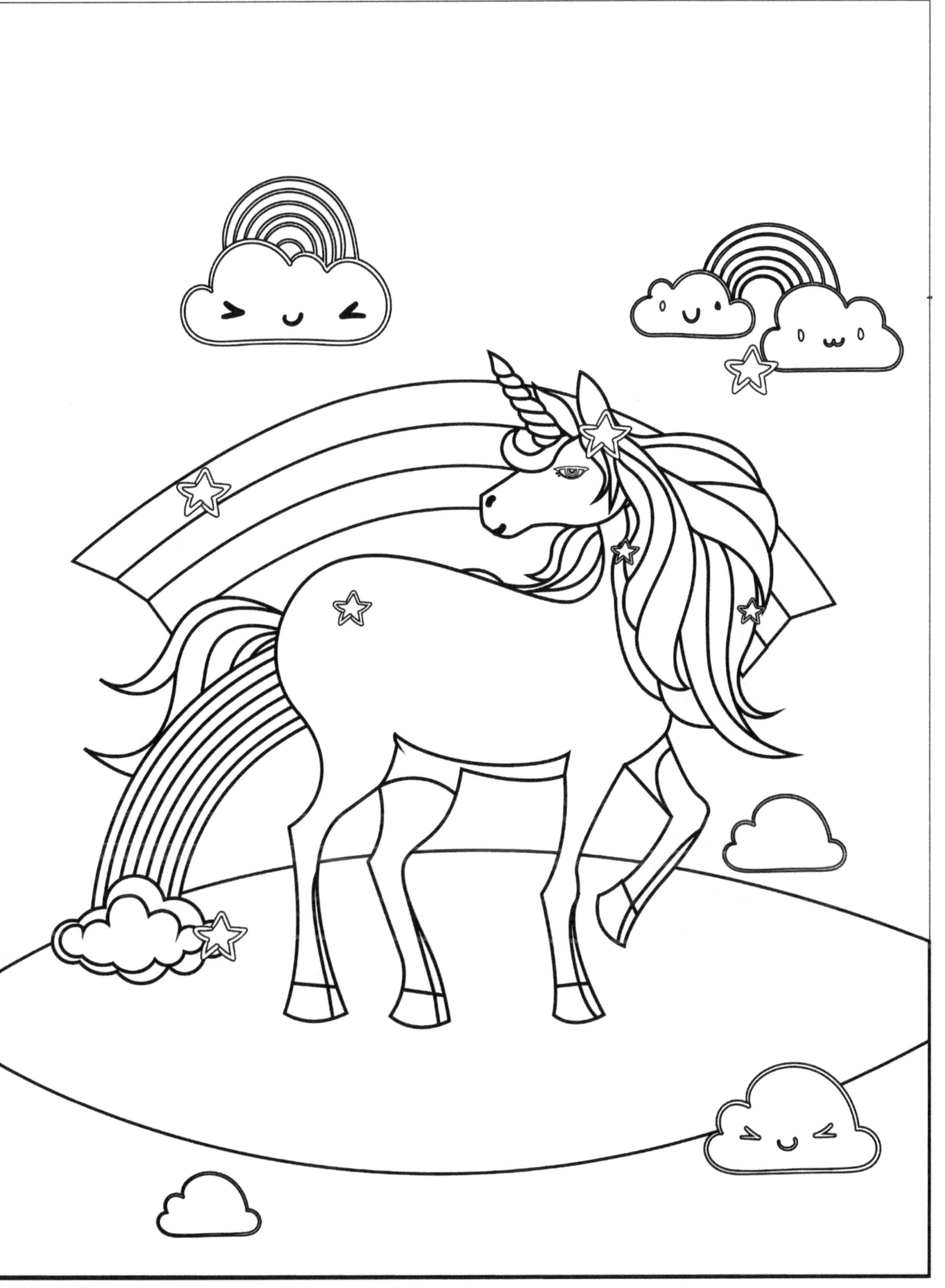

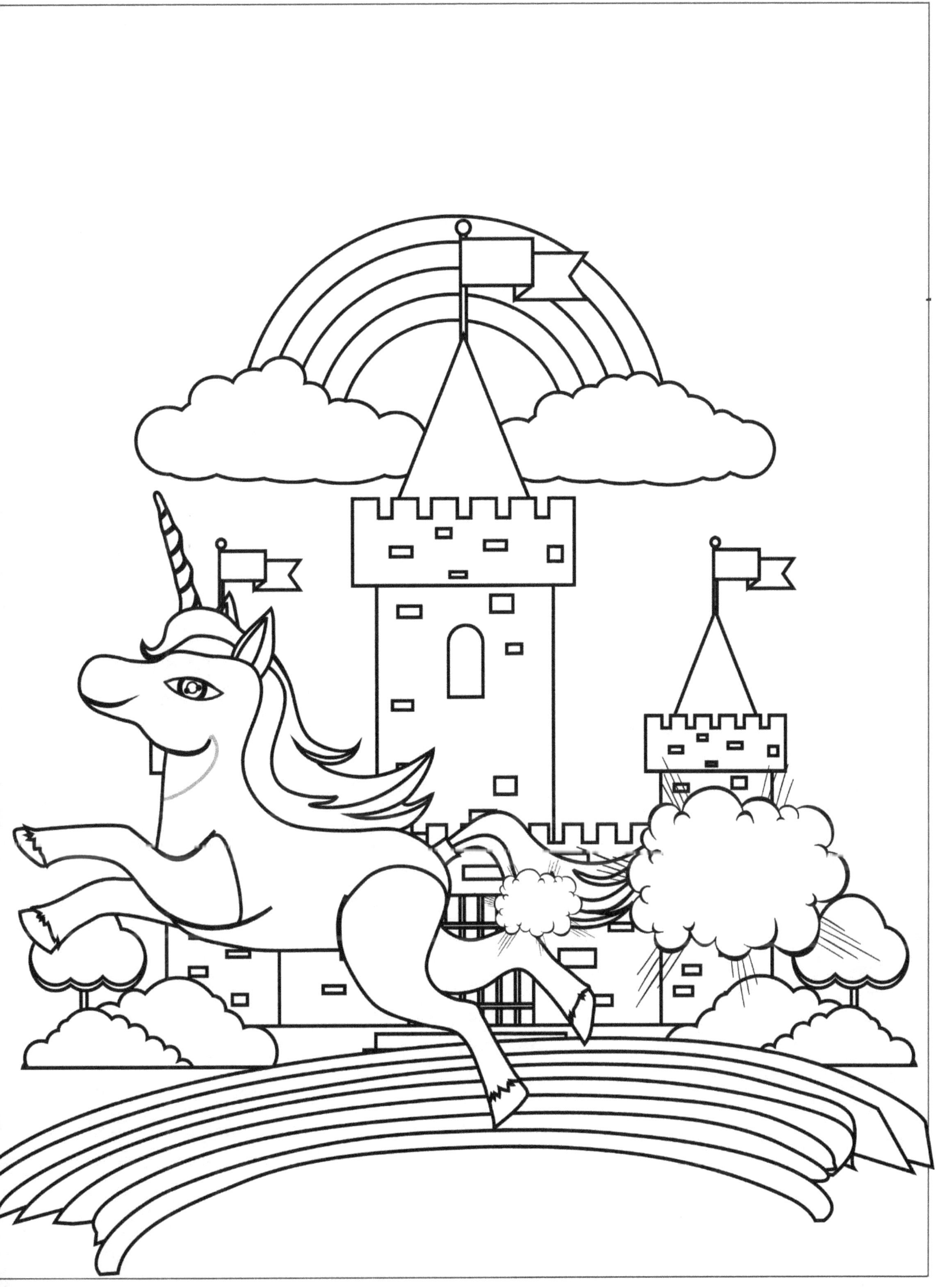

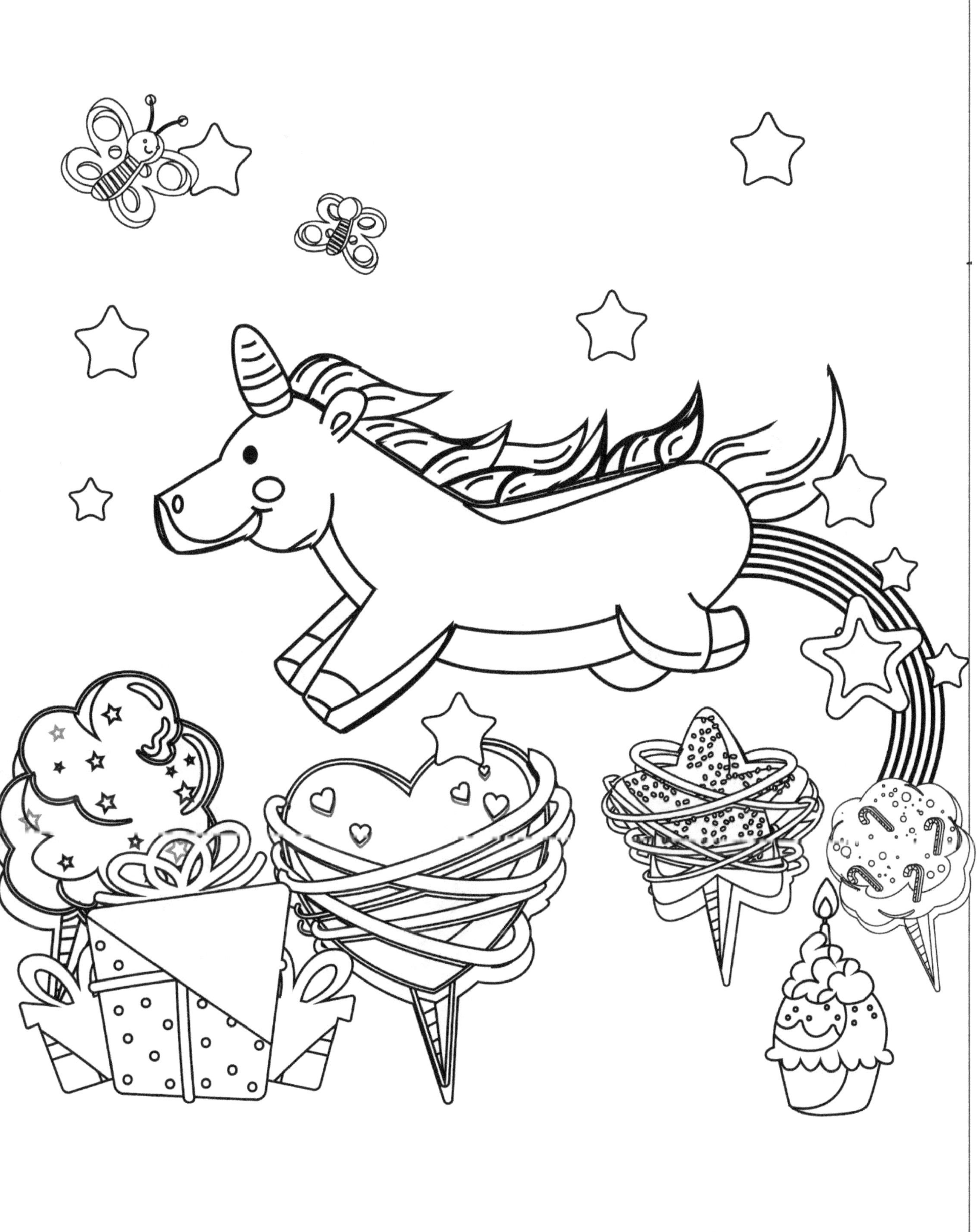

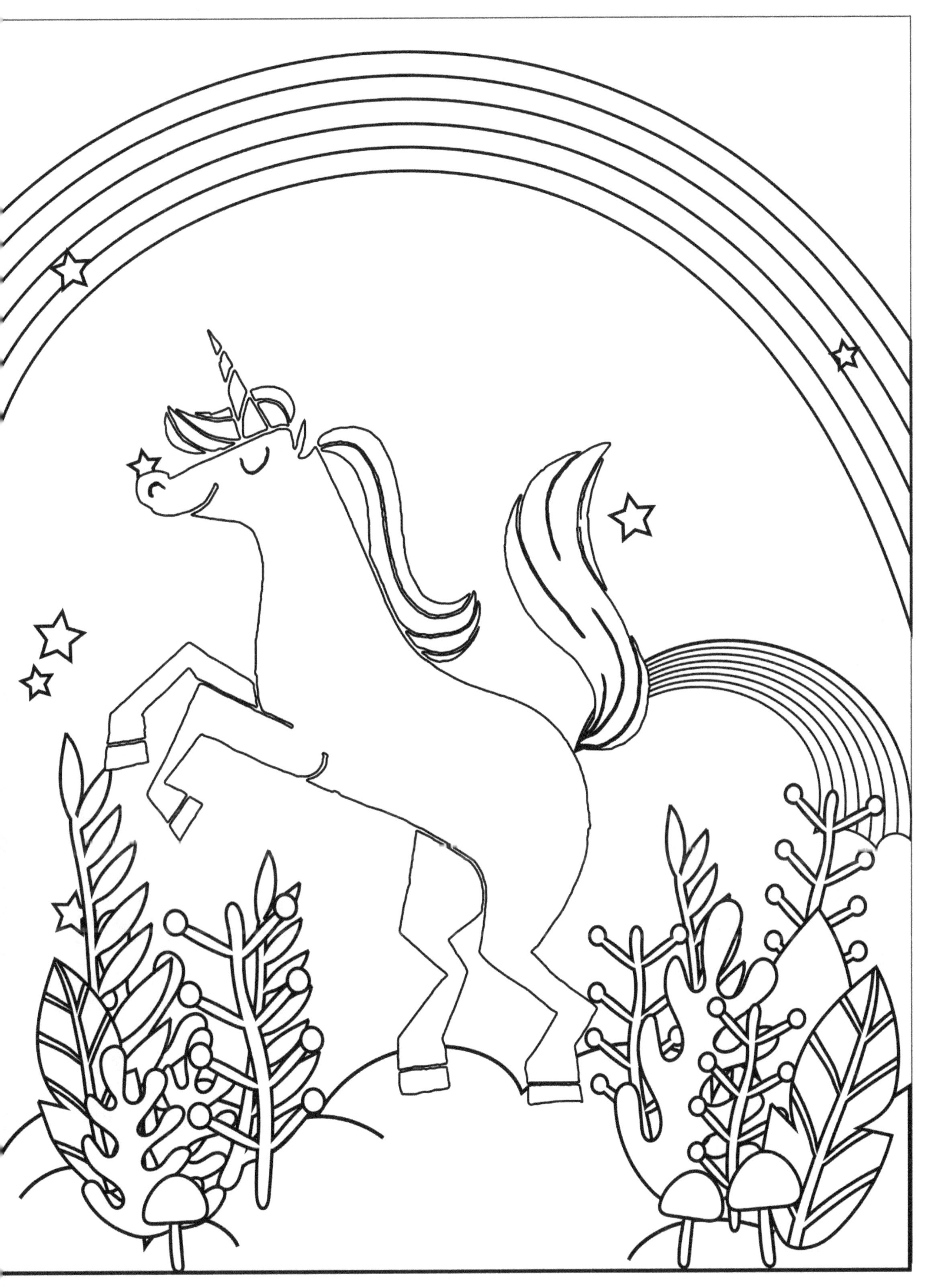

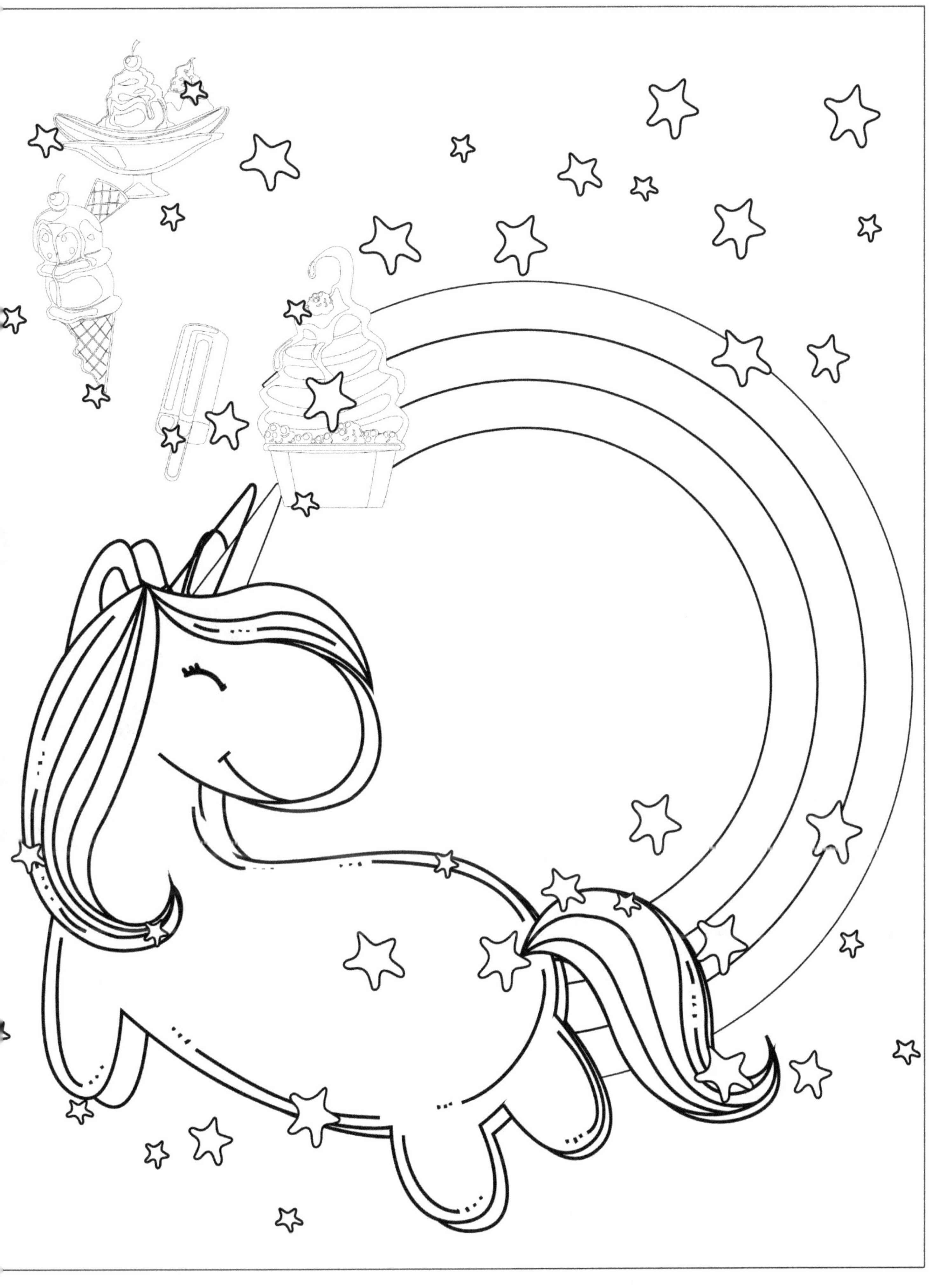

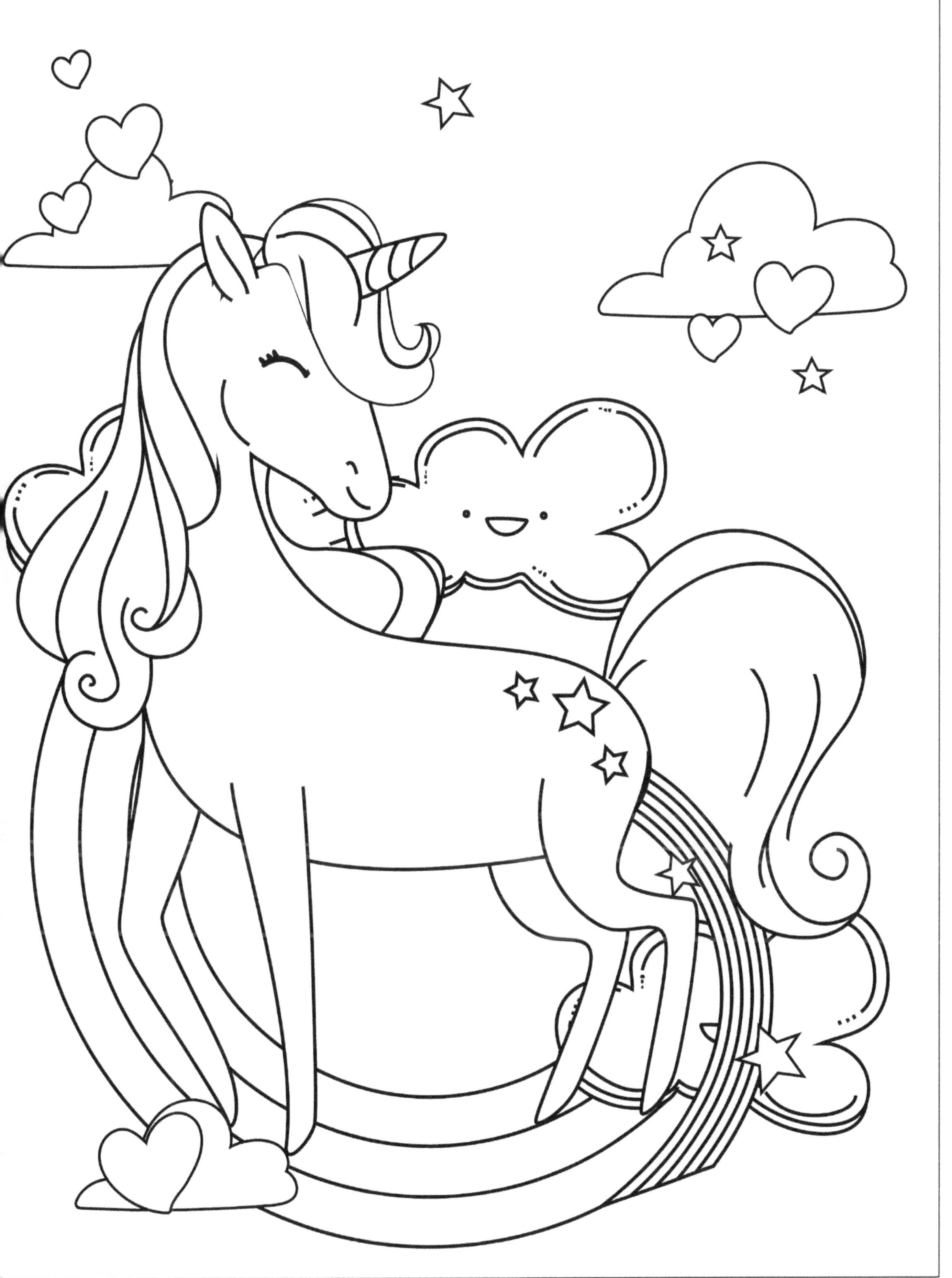

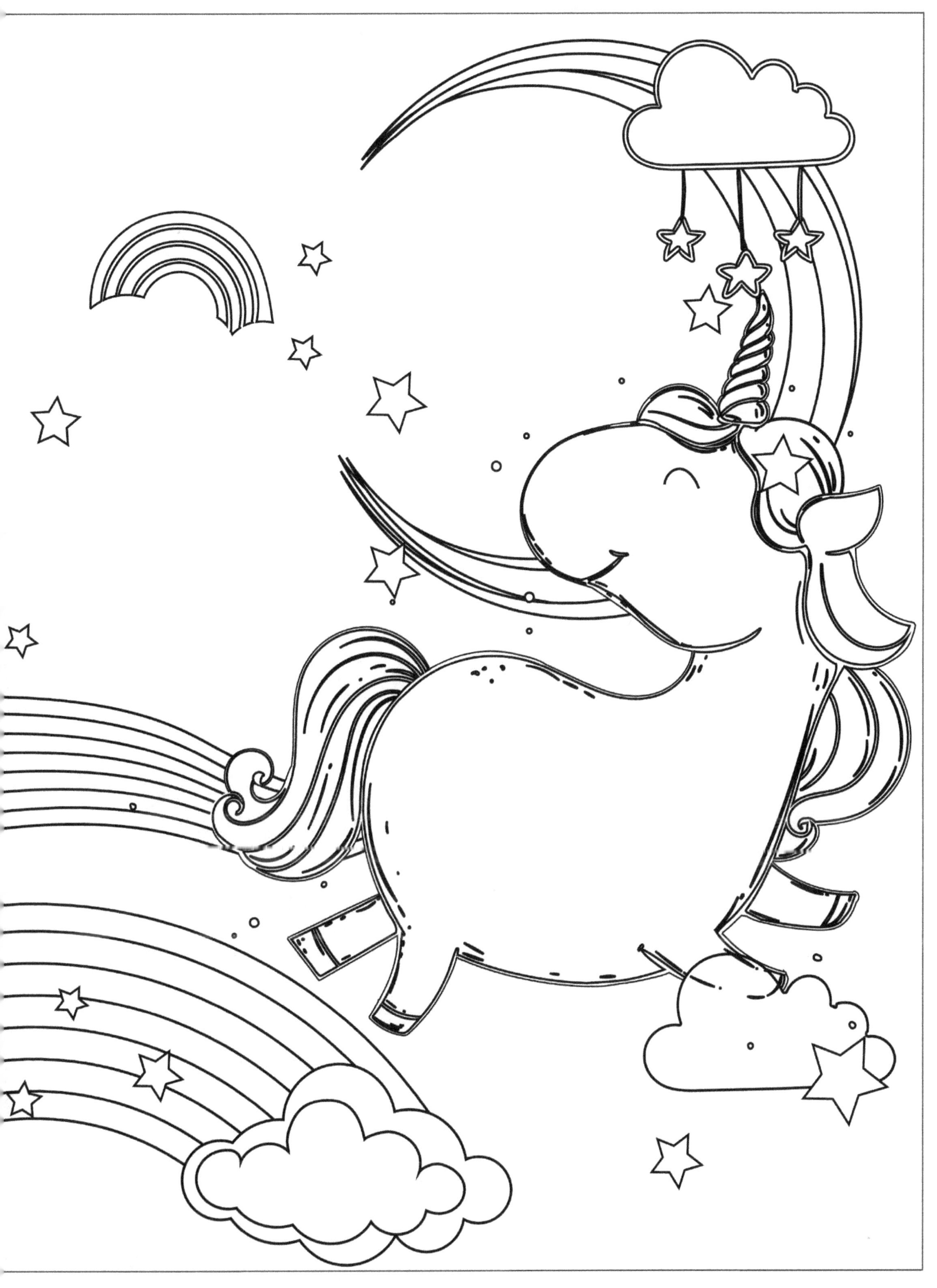

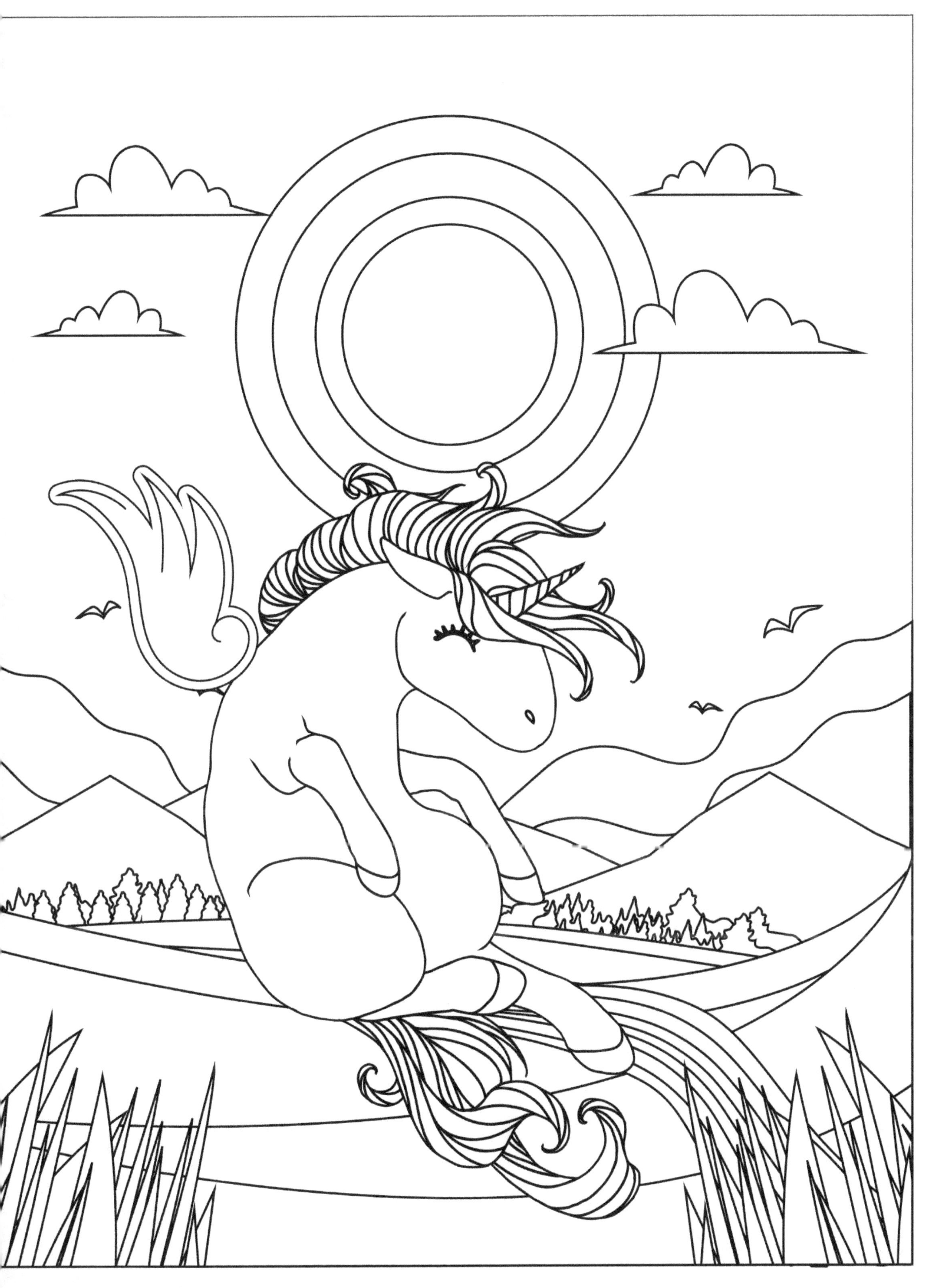

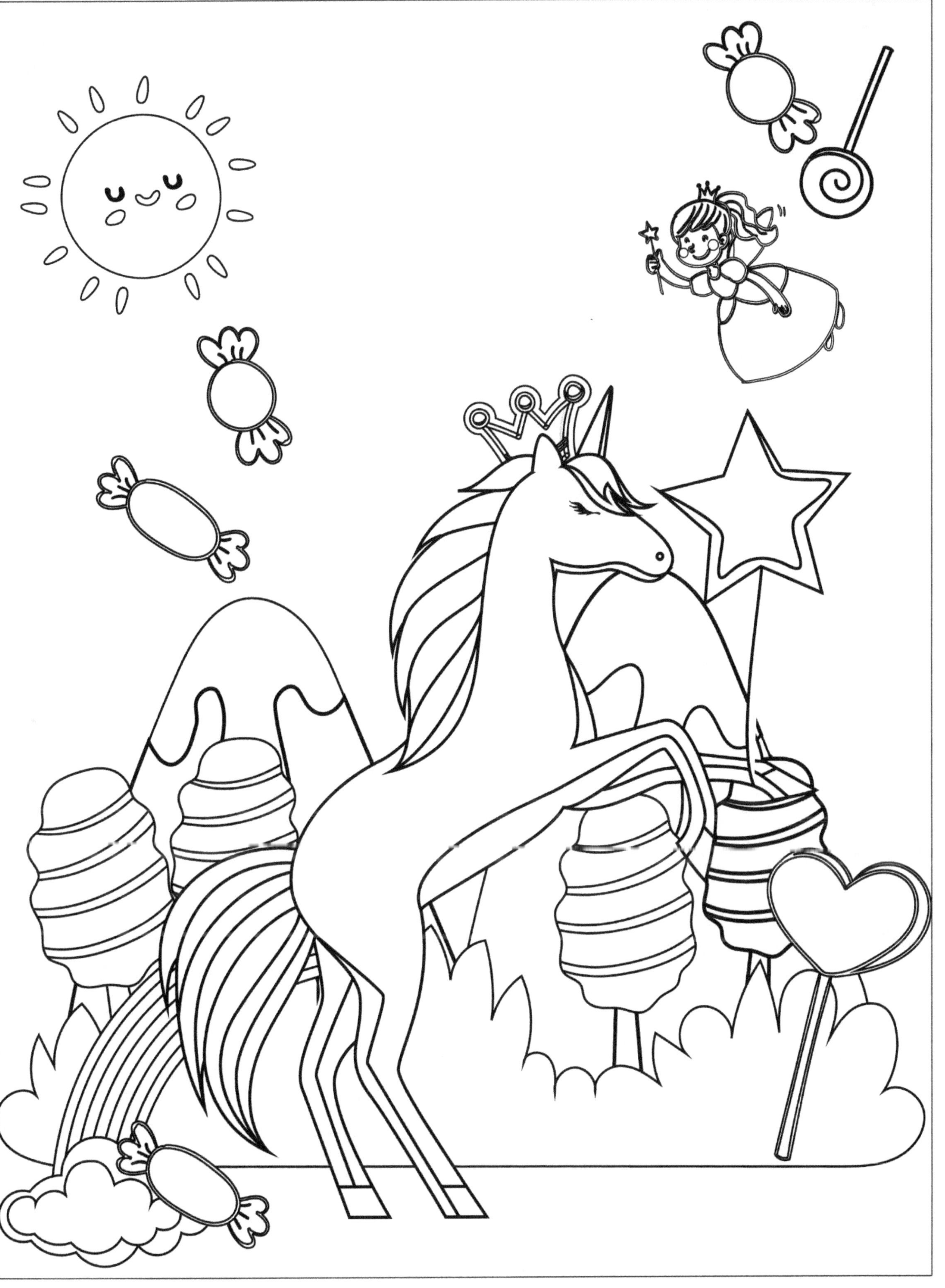

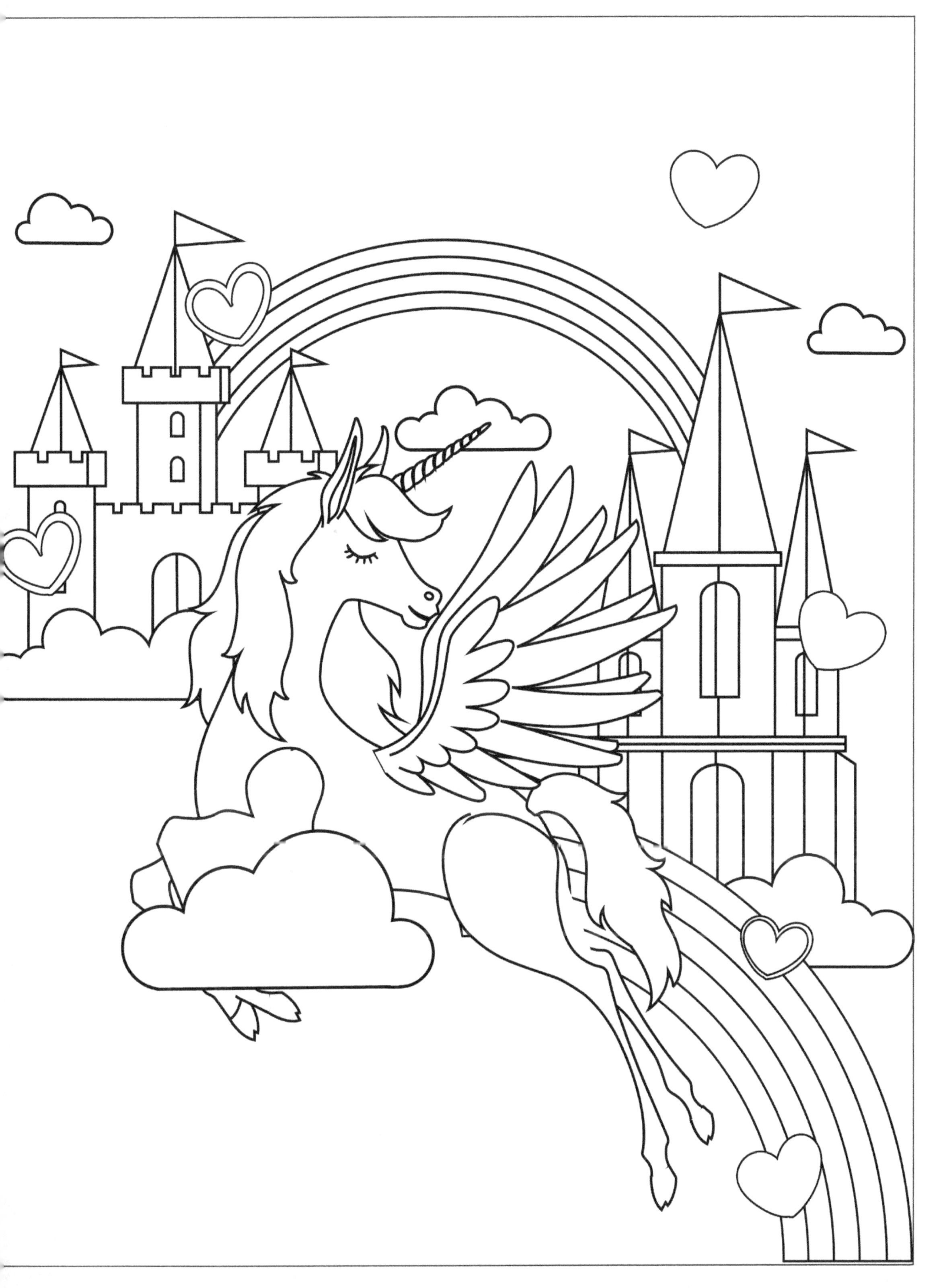

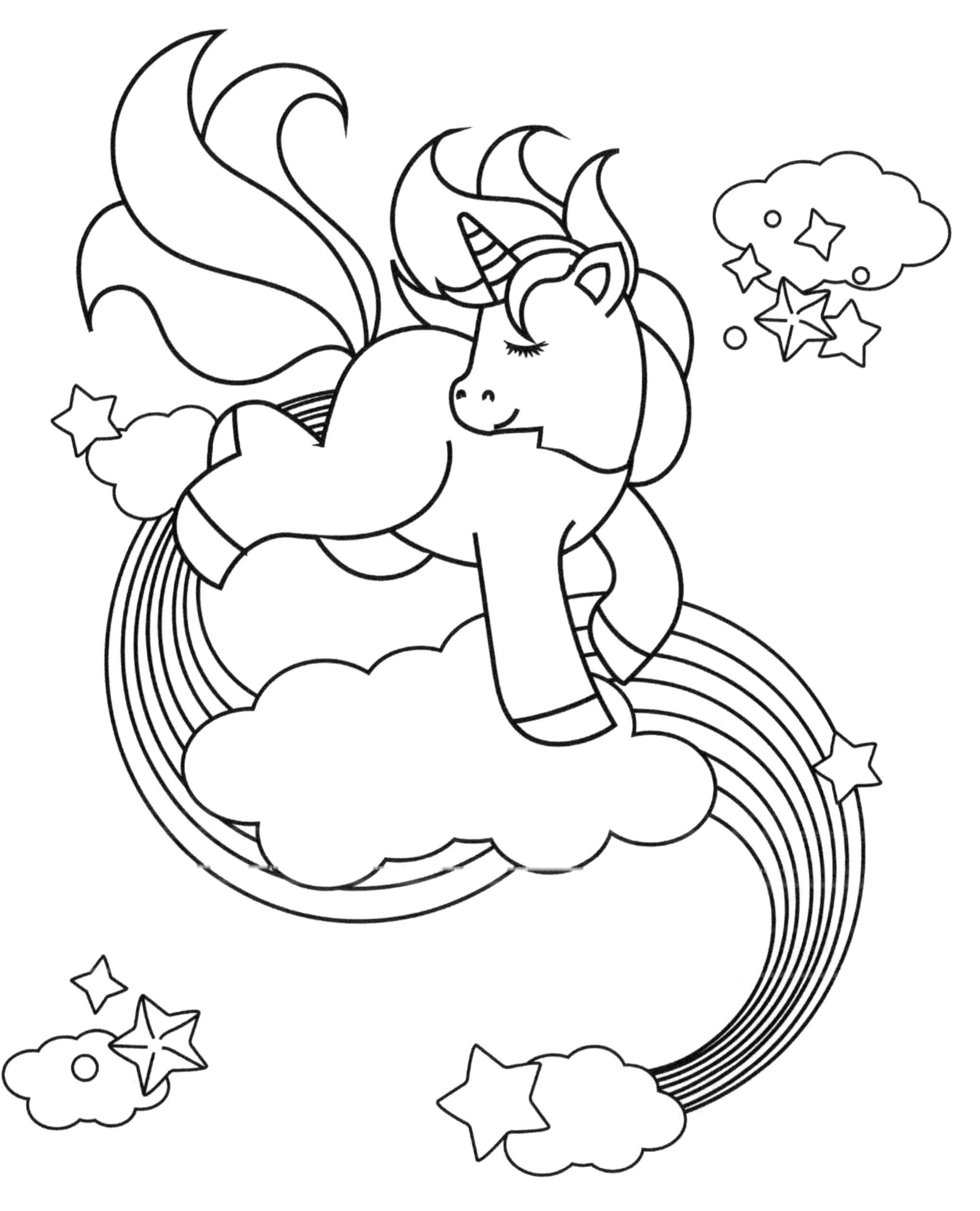

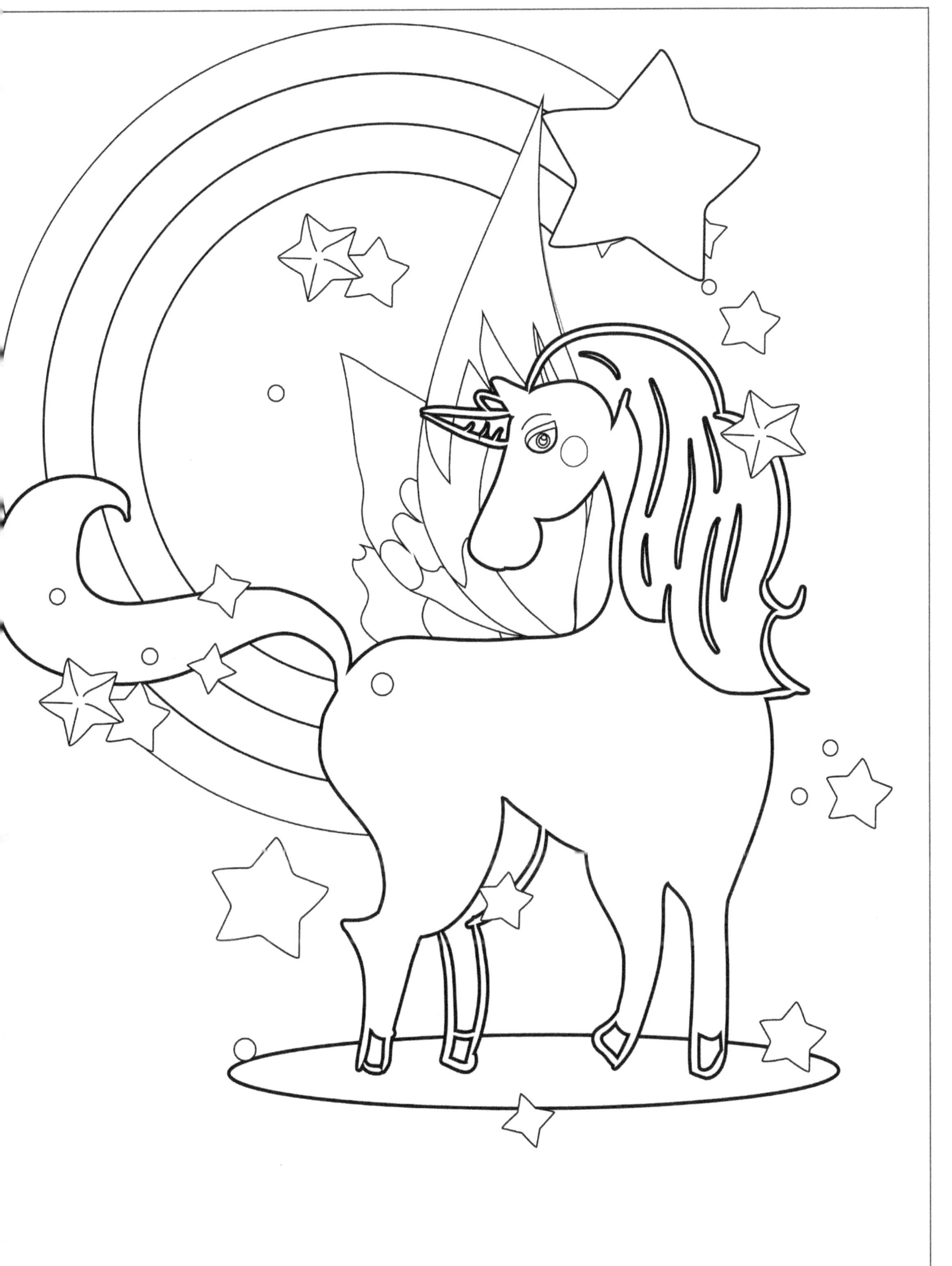

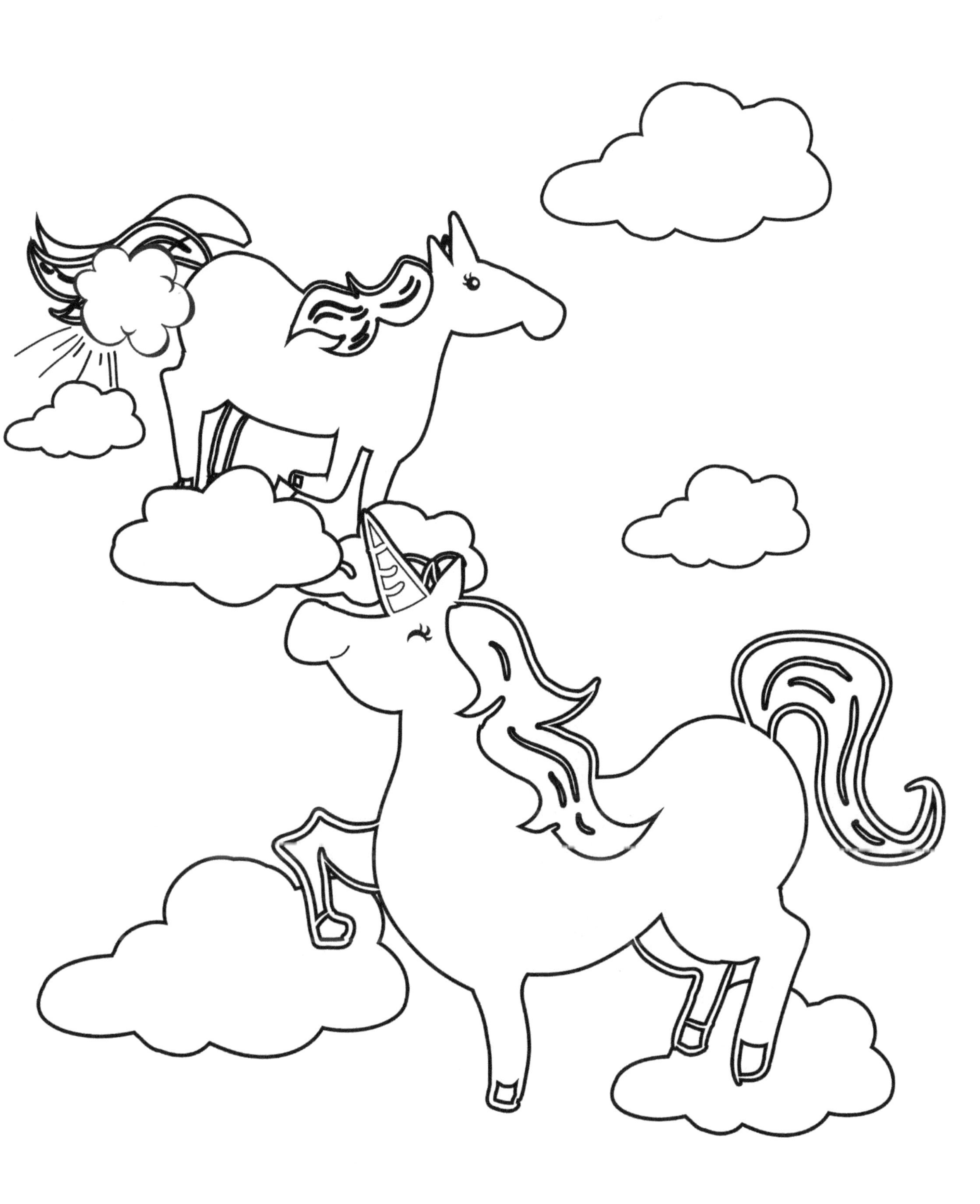

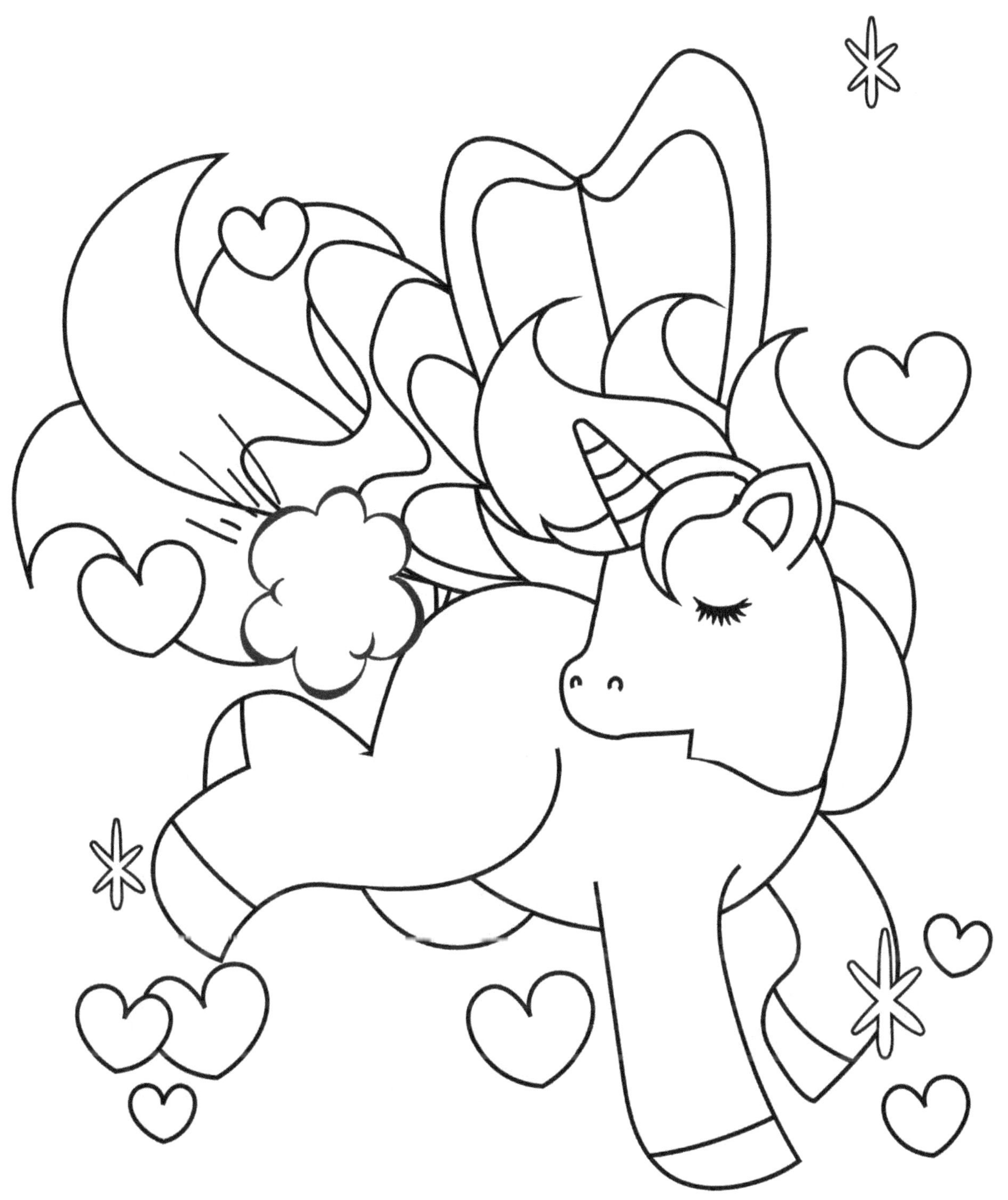

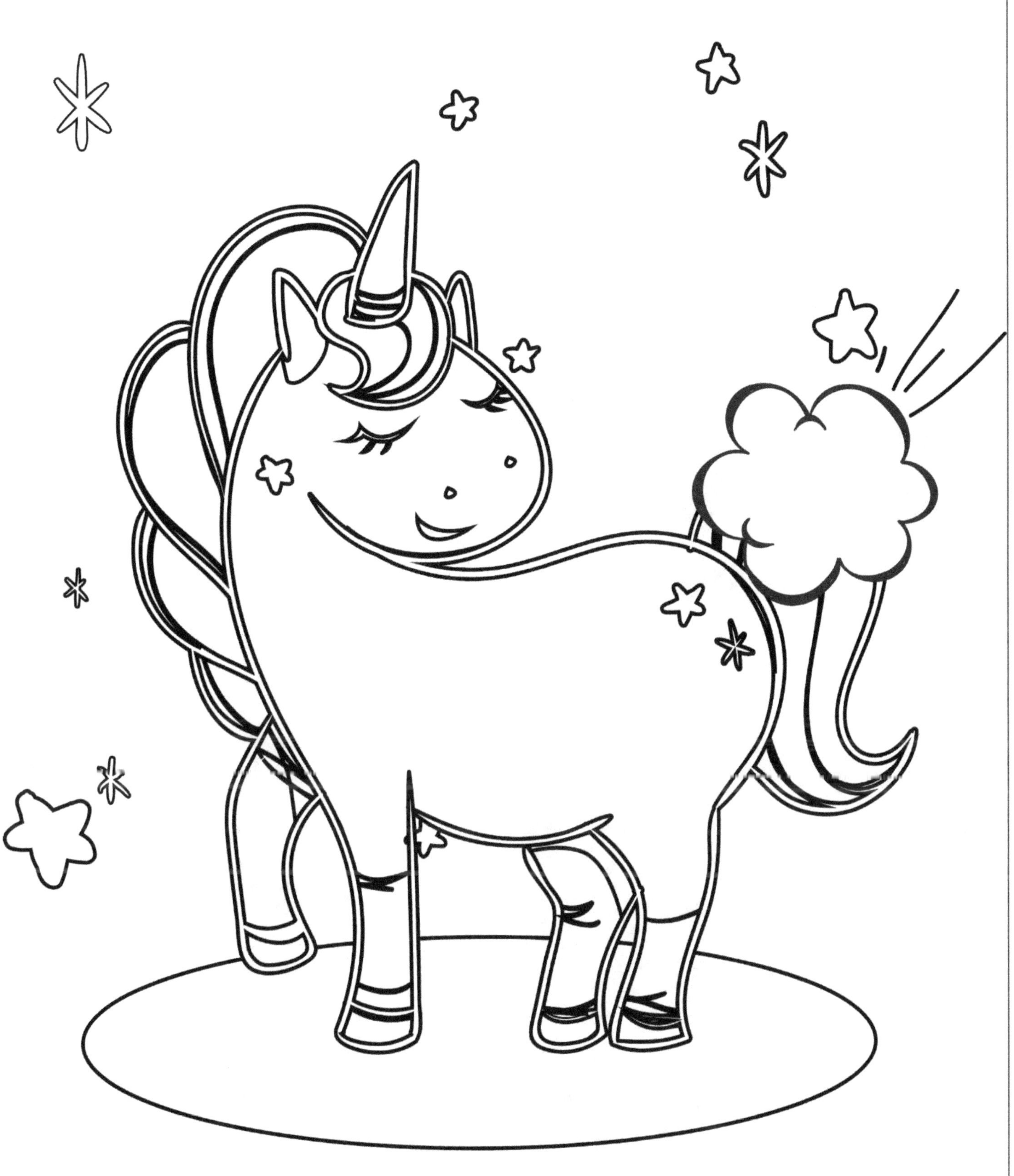

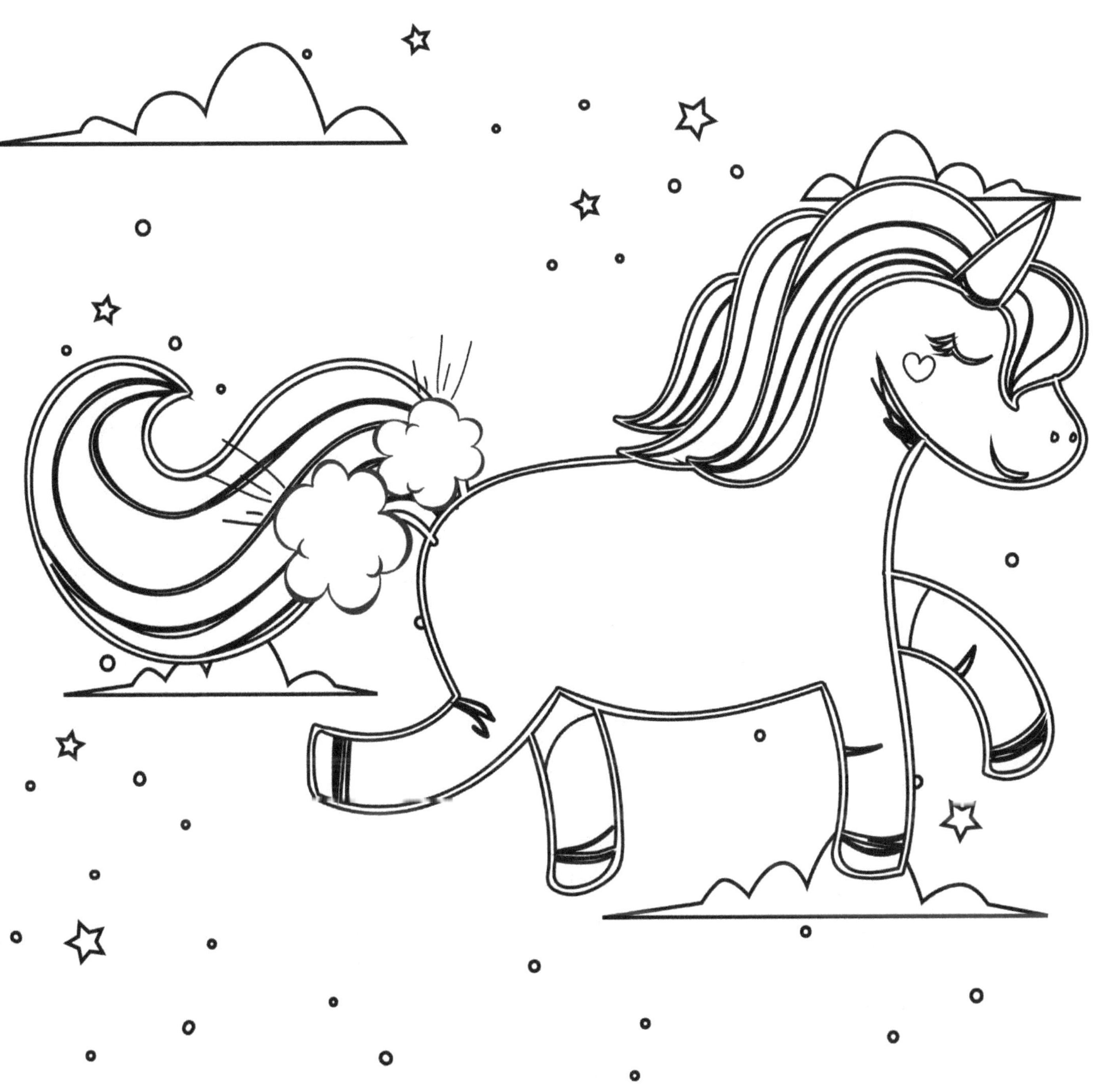

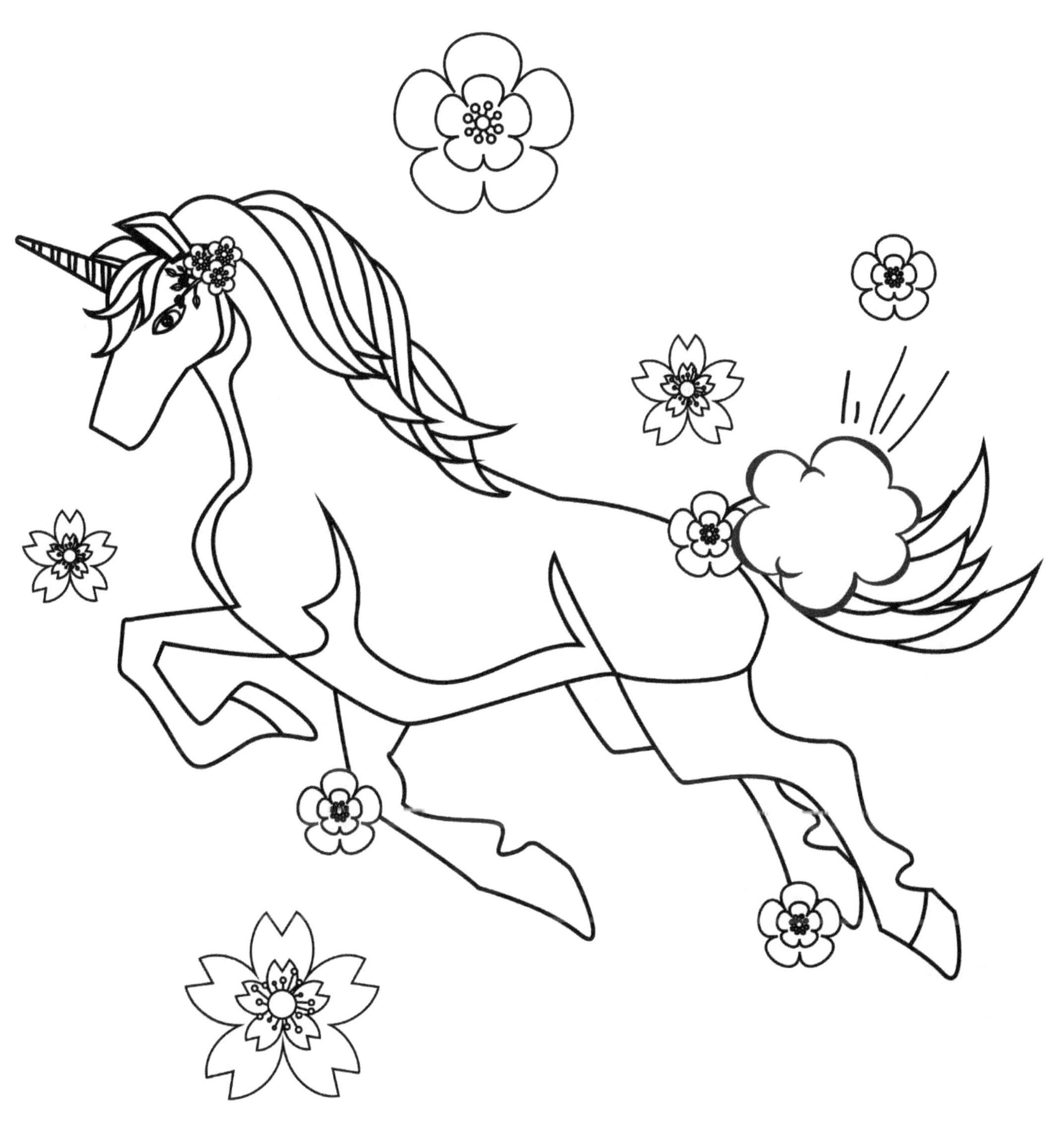

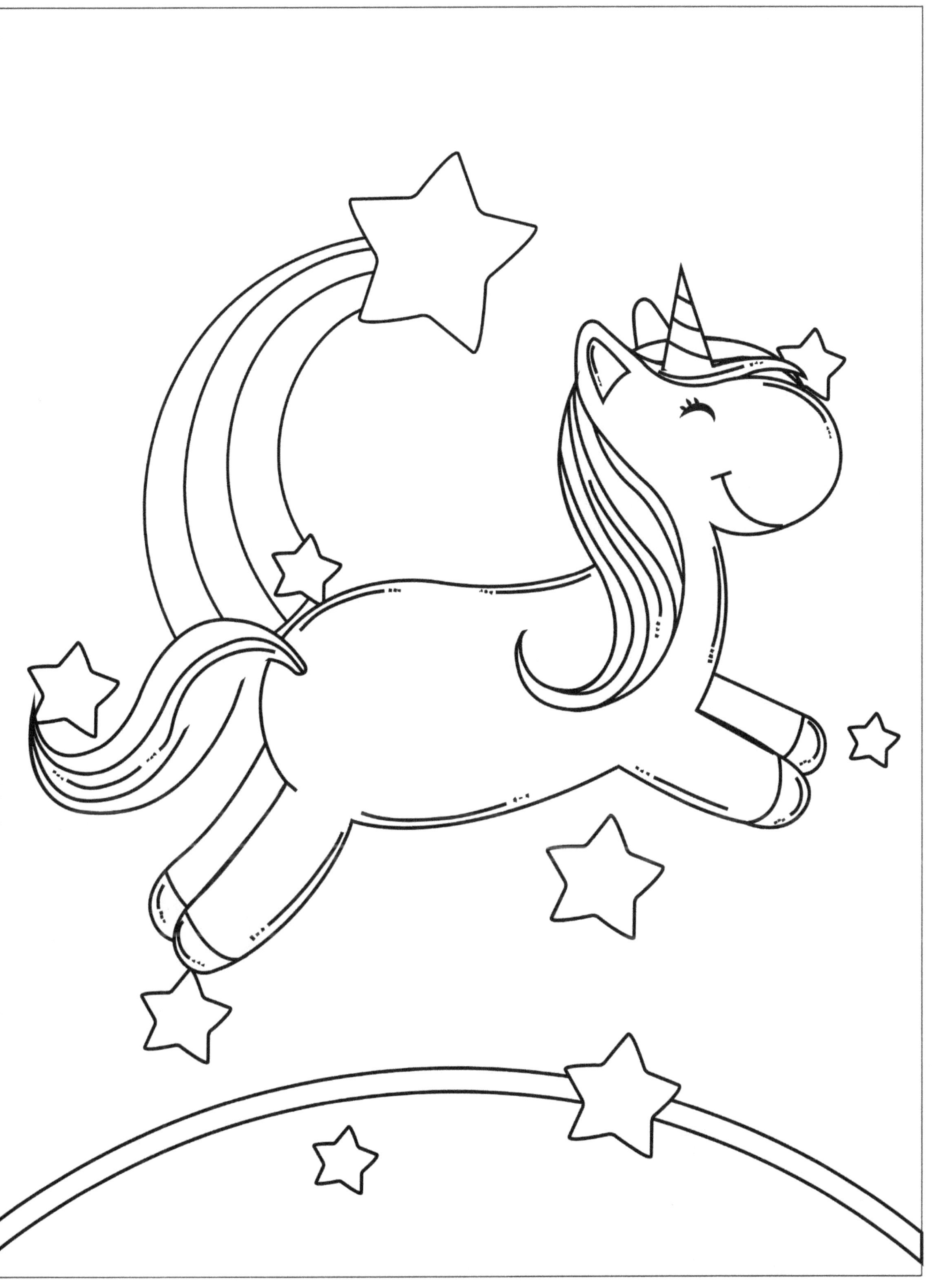

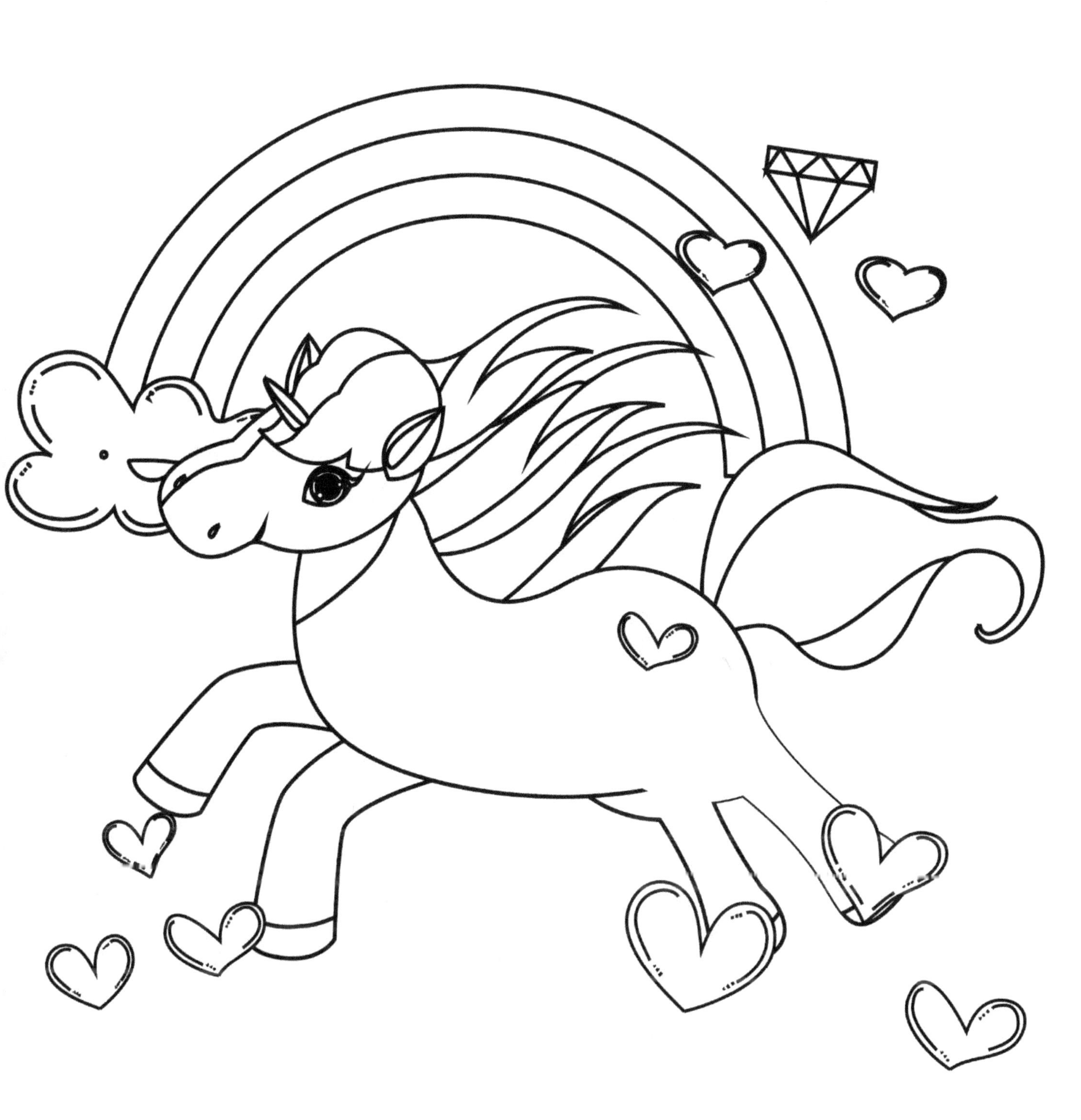

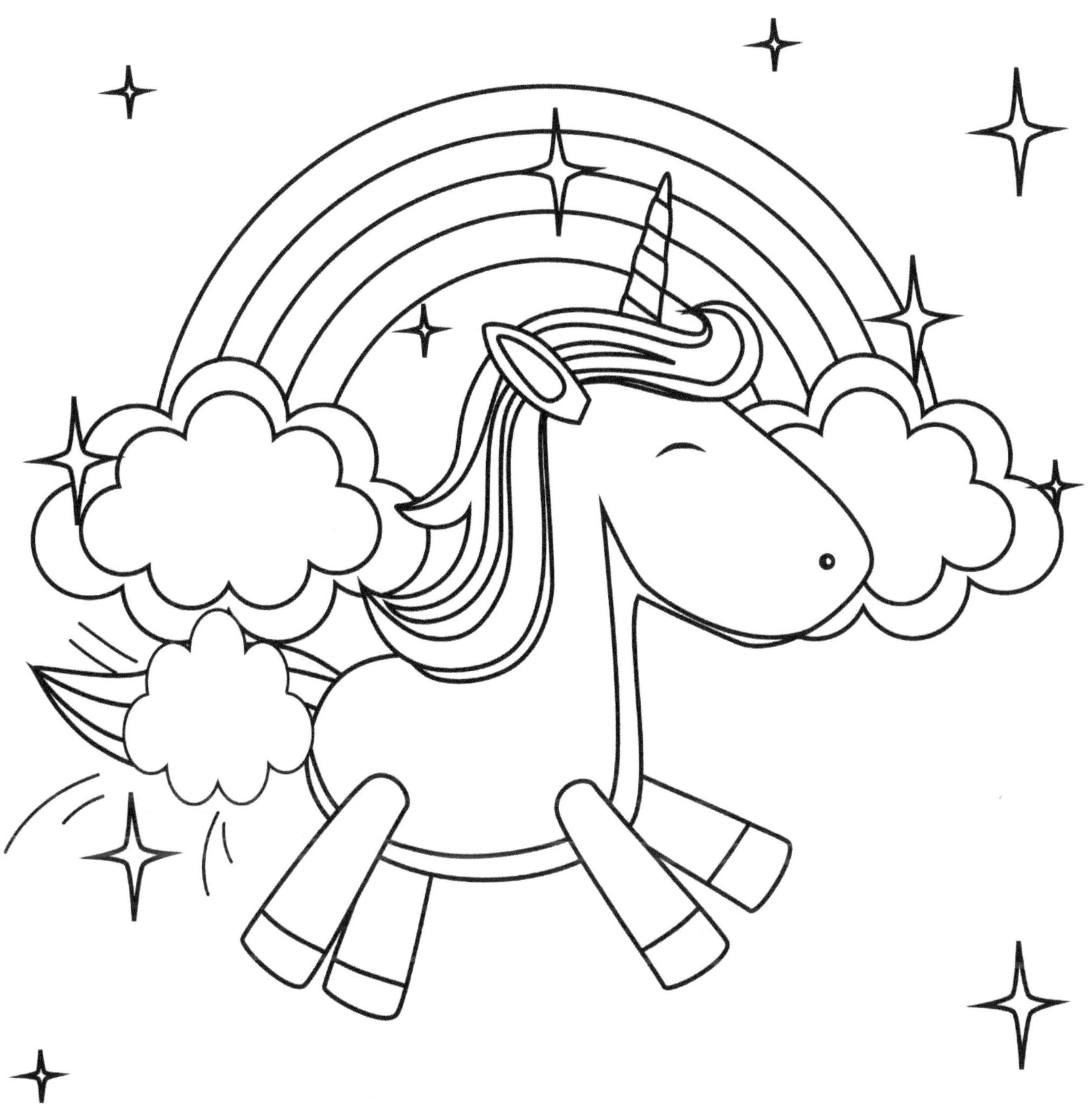

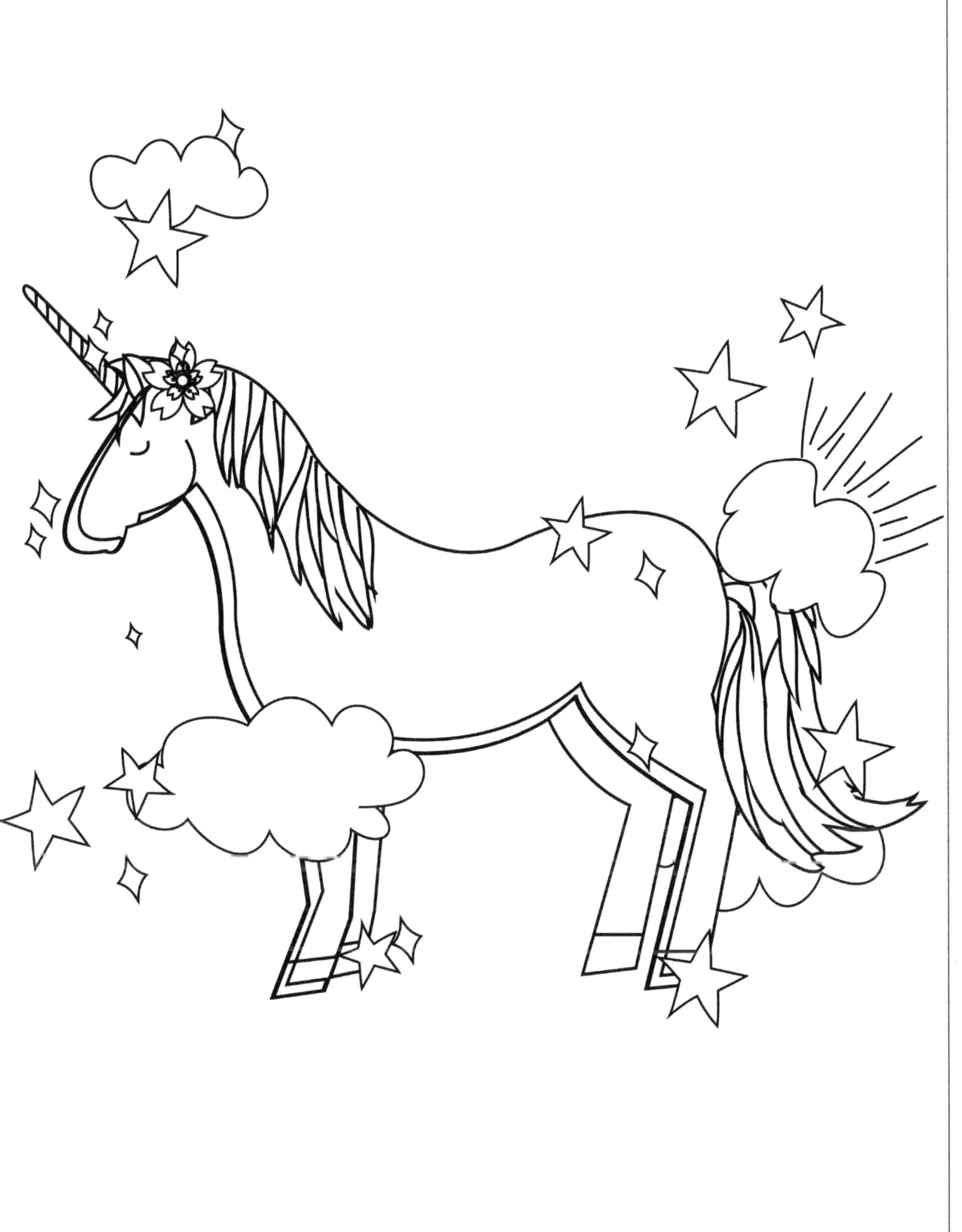

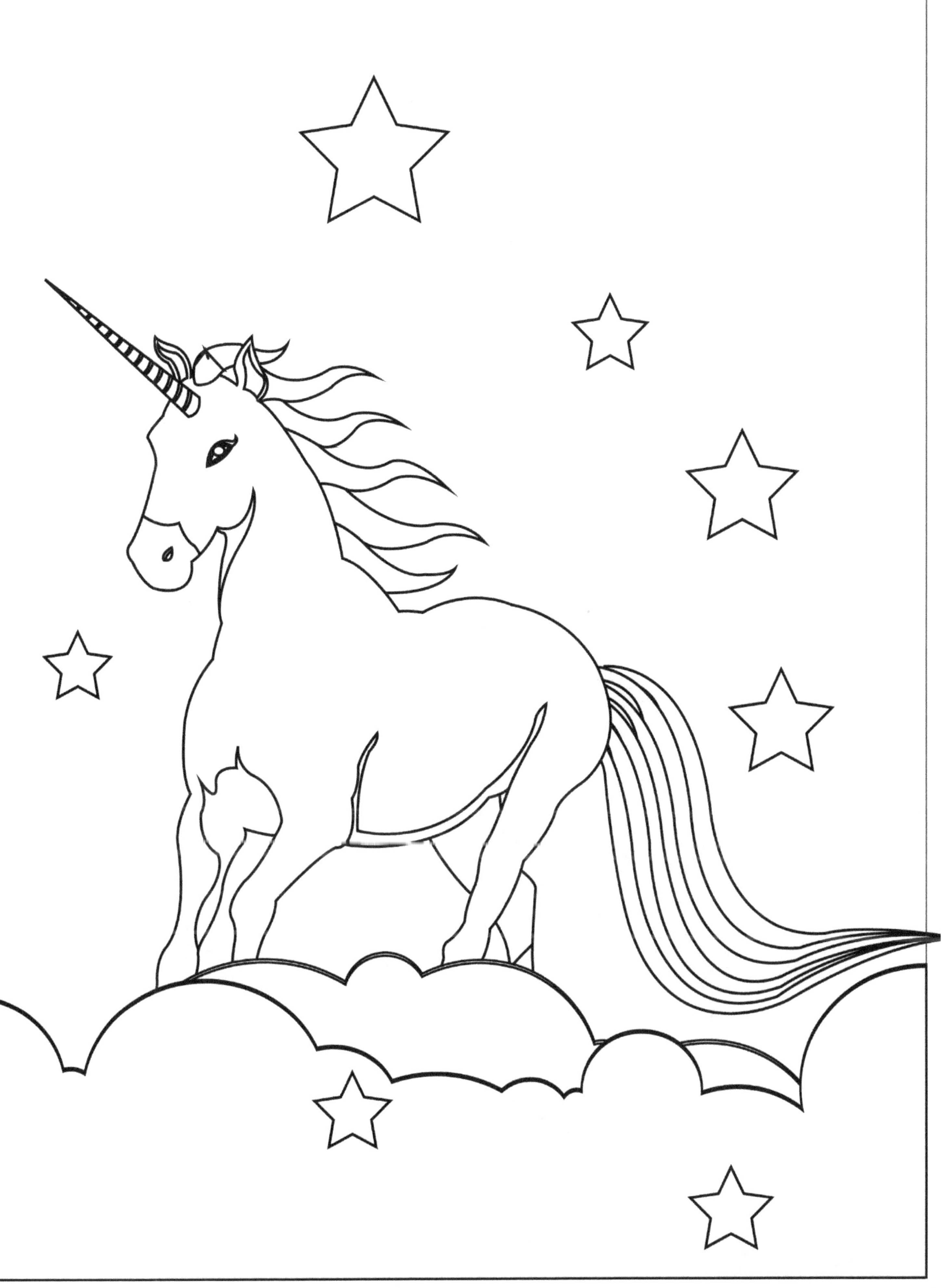

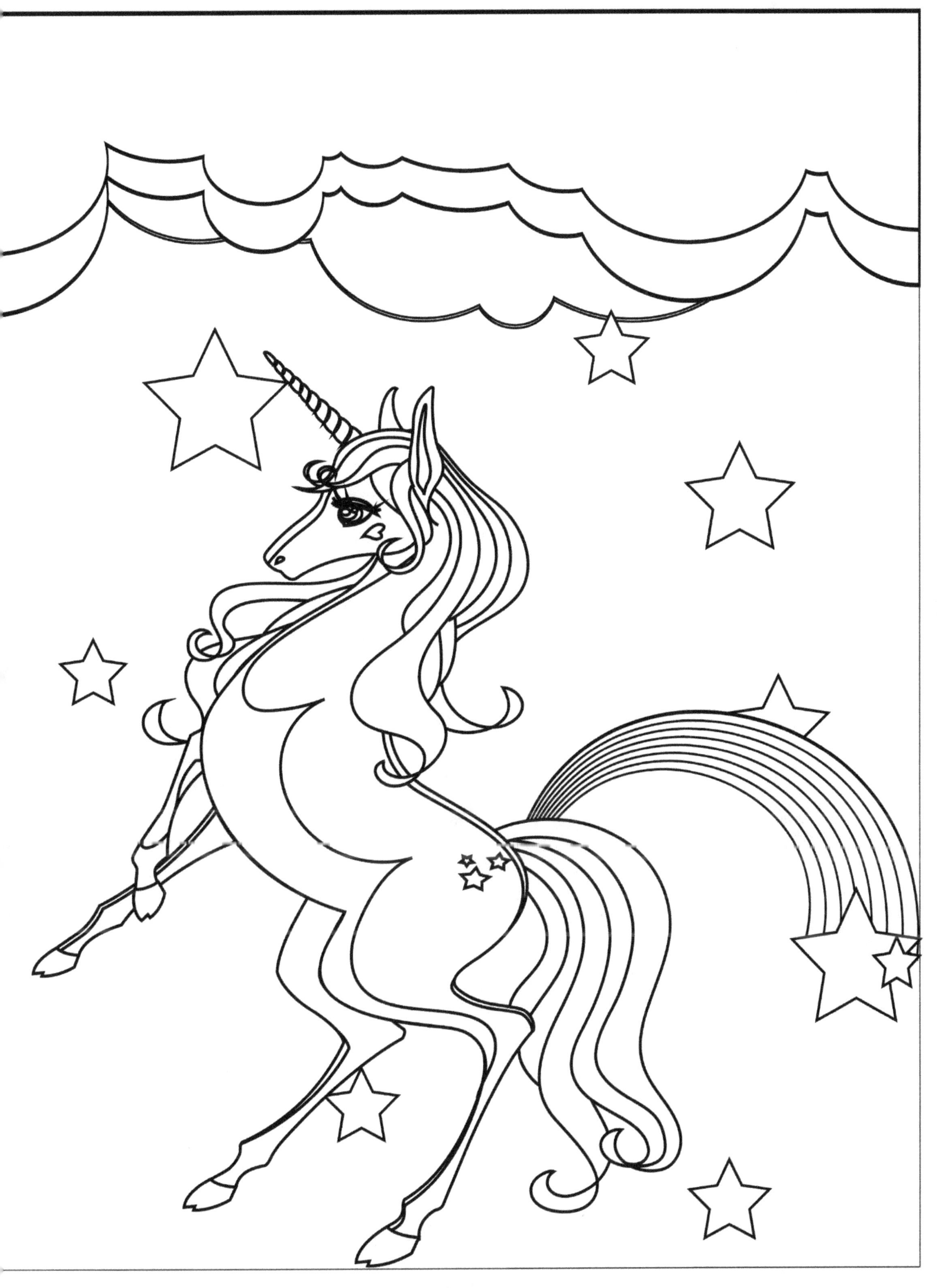

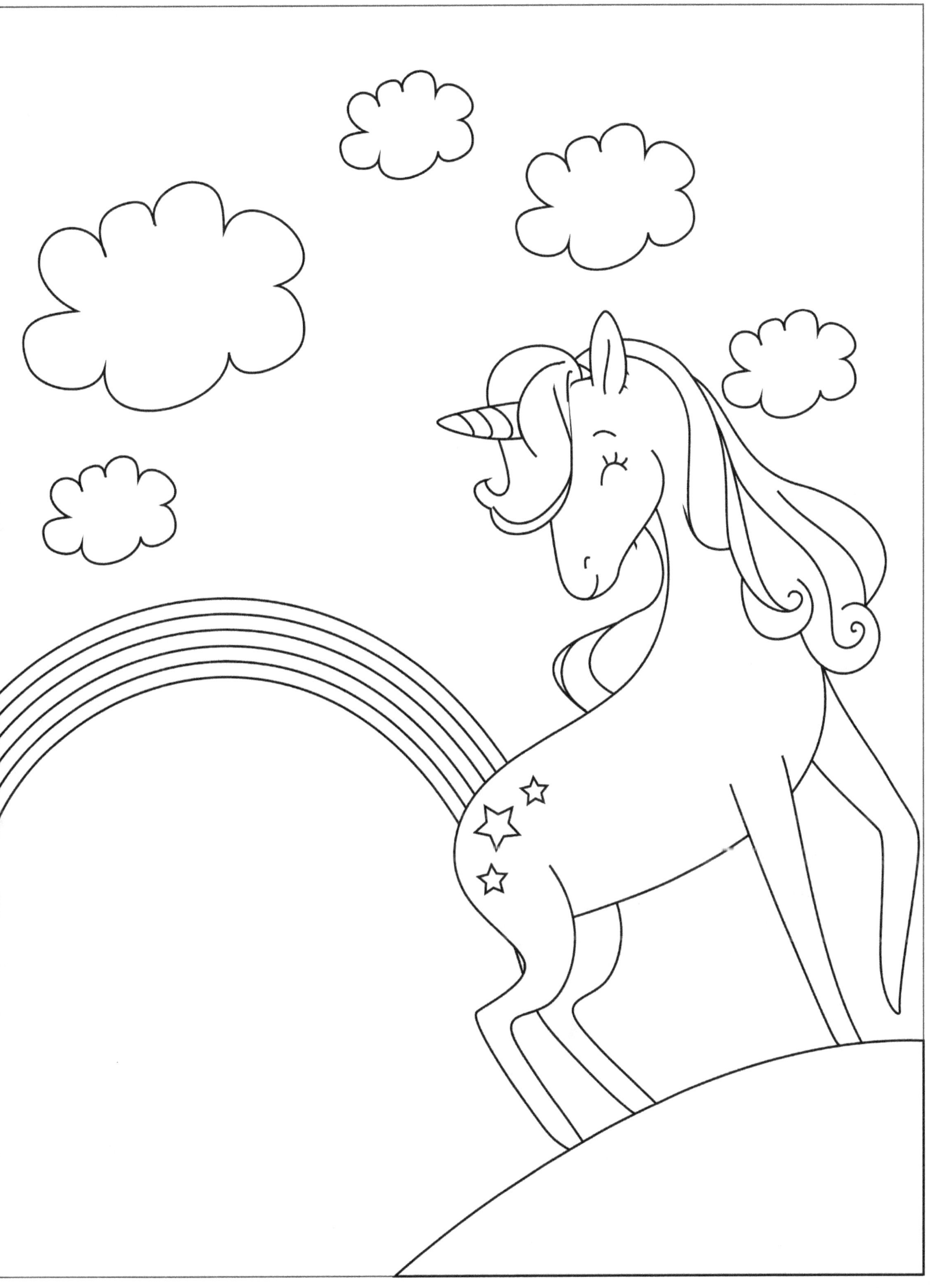

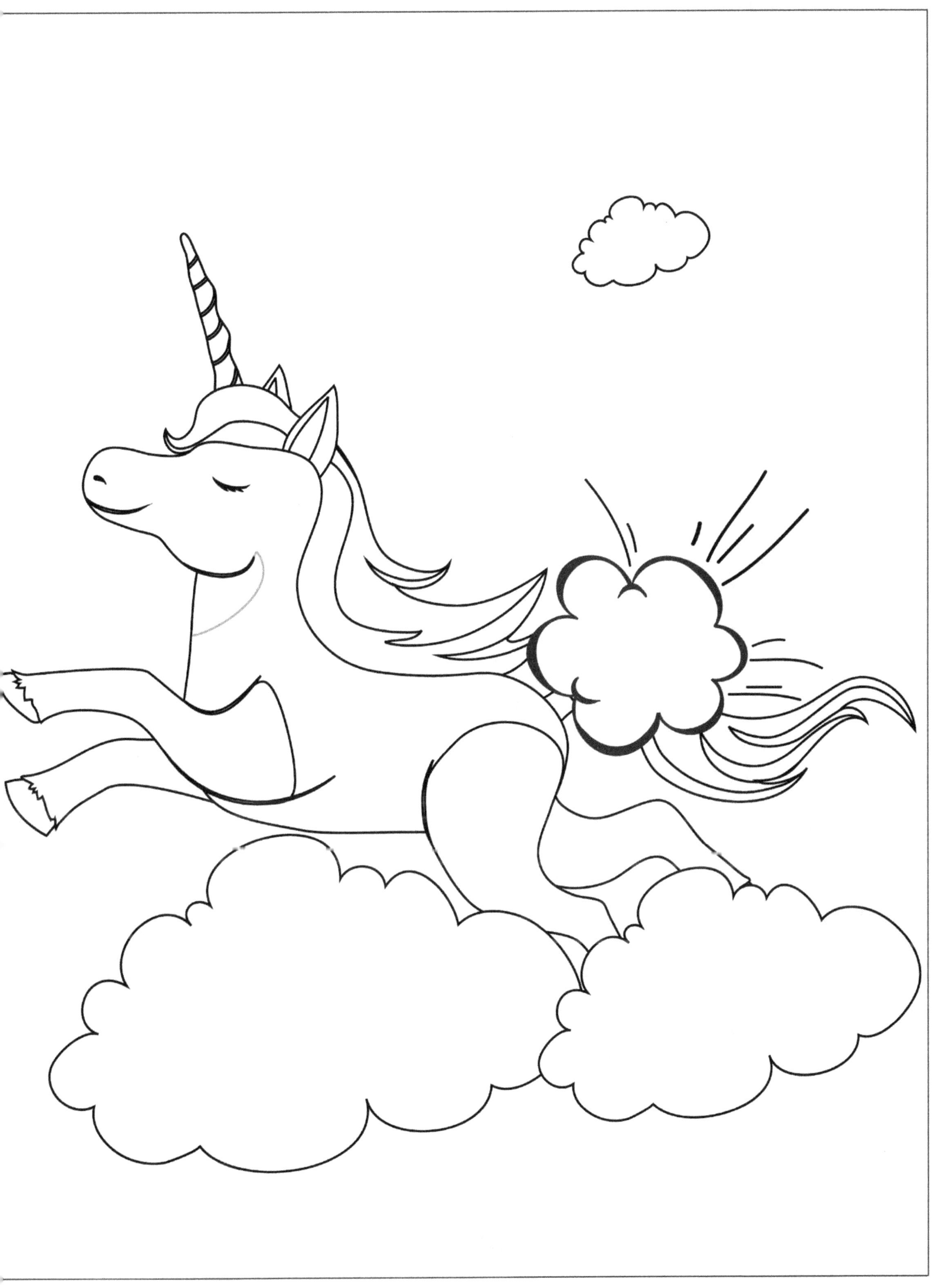

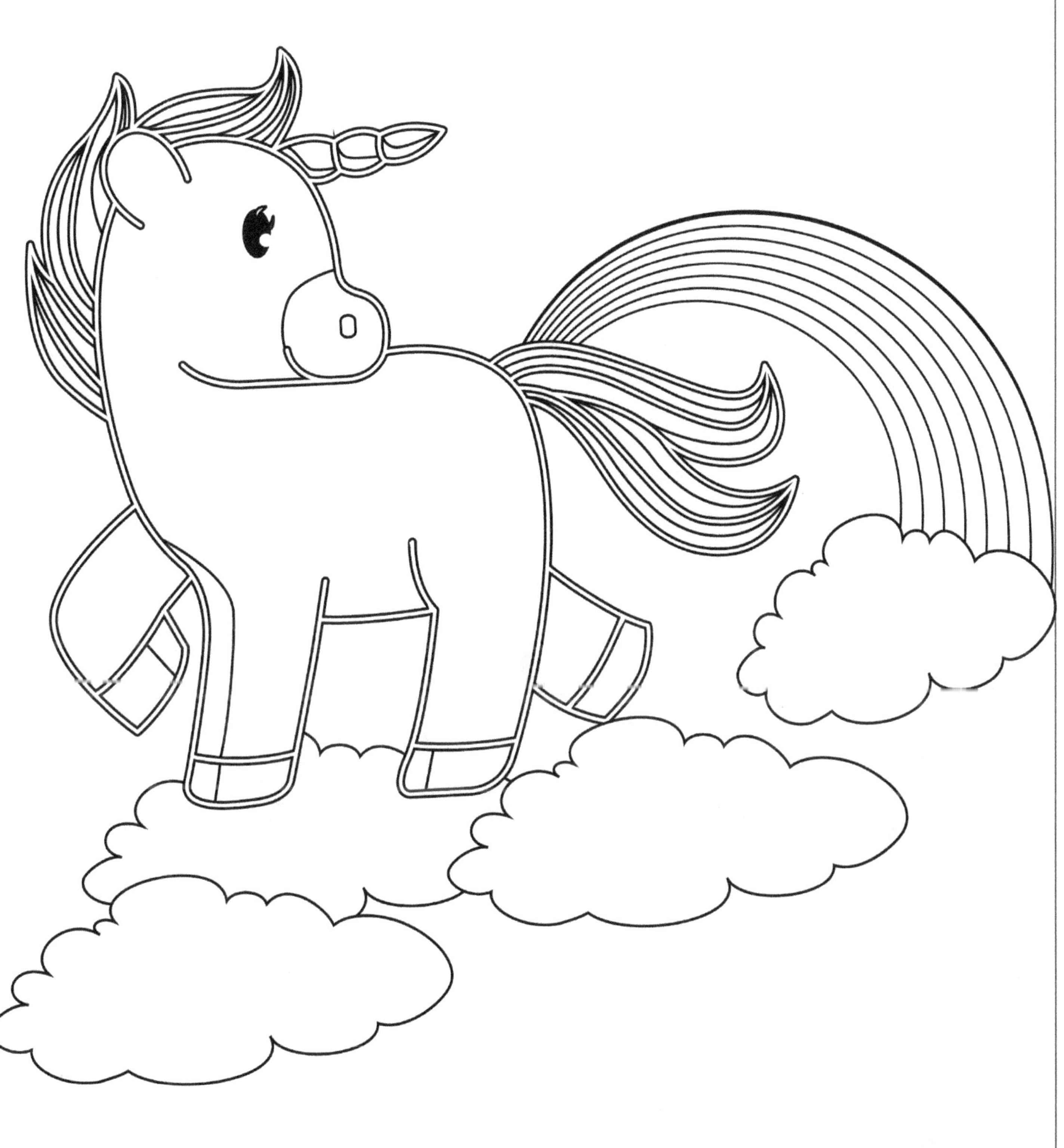

Bonus

www.ingramcontent.com/pod-product-compliance
Lightning Source LLC
Chambersburg PA
CBHW080840240525
27224CB00030B/673

* 9 7 8 1 9 7 5 7 8 7 4 1 7 *